access to history

RACE RELATIONS IN THE USA SINCE 1900

Vivienne Sanders

Hodder & Stoughton

A MEMBER OF THE HODDER HEADLINE GROUP

Acknowledgements

The front cover shows Martin Luther King reproduced courtesy of Associated Press.

The publishers would like to thank the following individuals, institutions and companies for permission to reproduce copyright illustrations in this book:
Associated Press/Jackson Daily News page 88; Associated Press AP page 92; Corbis pages 10, 39, 50 and 104; Corbis-Bettmann/UPI page 71; Hulton Getty page 33; Lifetime Books, Inc. page 4.

The publishers would also like to thank the following for permission to reproduce material in this book:
Cannongate Books Ltd for the extracts from *Let the Trumpet Sound* by S Oates, 1998; Copyright 1992, Holloway House Publishing Co., Los Angeles, California 90046 for the extracts from *Booker T Washington* by J Neyland, 1992; Macmillan Press Ltd for the extracts from *The Civil Rights Movement* by WTM Riches, Macmillan, 1997; Oxford University Press for the extracts from *Guns or Butter: The Presidency of Lyndon Johnson* by I Bernstein, 1996, *Booker T Washington: Up from Slavery*, 1995, *Lone Star Rising: Lyndon Johnson and his Times 1908–1960* by R Dallek, 1991 and *Flawed Giant: Lyndon Johnson and his Times 1961–1973* by R Dallek, 1998; Extracts from *500 Nations* by Alvin M Josephy, used courtesy of Pathways Productions, Inc. All rights reserved. Copyright 1994; Pearson Education Limited for the extracts from *Kennedy* by H Brogan, Longman, 1996, *Black Leadership in America* by J White, Longman, 1994 and *Sweet Land of Liberty?* by R Cook, Longman, 1998; The McGraw-Hill Companies for the extracts from *From Slavery to Freedom* by J Franklin, McGraw-Hill, 1998; Mercer University Press for the extract from *James F. Byrnes of South Carolina: A Remembrance* by Walter J. Brown, 1990; From *The Free and the Unfree* by Peter Carroll and David W Noble, copyright © 1977, 1988 by Peter N Carroll and David W Noble. Used by permission of Viking Penguin, a division of Penguin Putnam Inc.; The Random House Group Ltd for the extracts from *Bearing the Cross* by D Garrow, Jonathan Cape, 1993; Simon & Schuster for extracts from *Truman* by David McCullough, © 1992 by David McCullough; The University of Chicago Press for the extracts from *American Indians* by William T Hagan, 1993; The University of Oklahoma Press for the extract from *A History of the Indians of the United States* by A Debo, Pimlico, 1995; Nancy Gallagher, excerpt from *Breeding Better Vermonters* © 1999 by Nancy Gallagher, reprinted by permission of University Press of New England.

Every effort has been made to trace and acknowledge ownership of copyright. The publishers will be glad to make suitable arrangements with any copyright holders whom it has not been possible to contact.

Orders: please contact Bookpoint Ltd, 78 Milton Park, Abingdon, Oxon OX14 4TD. Telephone: (44) 01235 827720, Fax: (44) 01235 400454. Lines are open from 9.00–6.00, Monday to Saturday, with a 24 hour message answering service. Email address: orders@bookpoint.co.uk

British Library Cataloguing in Publication Data
A catalogue record for this title is available from The British Library

ISBN 0 340 75345 5

First published 2000
Impression number 10 9 8 7 6 5 4 3 2 1
Year 2005 2004 2003 2002 2001 2000

Copyright © 2000 Vivienne Sanders

Typeset by Fakenham Photosetting Ltd, Fakenham, Norfolk.
Printed in Great Britain for Hodder & Stoughton Educational, a division of Hodder Headline Plc, 338 Euston Road, London NW1 3BH by Redwood Books, Trowbridge, Wilts.

Contents

Preface

To the general reader

Although the *Access to History* series has been designed with the needs of students studying the subject at higher examination levels very much in mind, it also has a great deal to offer the general reader. The main body of the text (i.e. ignoring the 'Study Guides' at the ends of chapters) forms a readable and yet stimulating survey of a coherent topic as studied by historians. However, each author's aim has not merely been to provide a clear explanation of what happened in the past (to interest and inform): it has also been assumed that most readers wish to be stimulated into thinking further about the topic and to form opinions of their own about the significance of the events that are described and discussed (to be challenged). Thus, although no prior knowledge of the topic is expected on the reader's part, she or he is treated as an intelligent and thinking person throughout. The author tends to share ideas and possibilities with the reader, rather than passing on numbers of so-called 'historical truths'.

To the student reader

This title ensures the results of recent research are reflected in the text and includes features aimed at assisting you in your study of the topic at AS level, A level and Higher. Two features are designed to assist you during your first reading of a chapter. The *Points to Consider* section following each chapter title is intended to focus your attention on the main theme(s) of the chapter, and the issues box following most section headings alerts you to the question or questions to be dealt with in the section. The *Working on . . .* section at the end of each chapter suggests ways of gaining maximum benefit from the chapter.

There are many ways in which the series can be used by students studying History at a higher level. It will, therefore, be worthwhile thinking about your own study strategy before you start your work on this book. Obviously, your strategy will vary depending on the aim you have in mind, and the time for study that is available to you.

If, for example, you want to acquire a general overview of the topic in the shortest possible time, the following approach will probably be the most effective:

1. Read chapter 1. As you do so, keep in mind the issues raised in the *Points to Consider* section.
2. Read the *Points to Consider* section at the beginning of chapter 2 and decide whether it is necessary for you to read this chapter.
3. If it is, read the chapter, stopping at each heading or sub-heading to

note down the main points that have been made. Often, the best way of doing this is to answer the question(s) posed in the Issues boxes.
4. Repeat stage 2 (and stage 3 where appropriate) for all the other chapters.

If, however, your aim is to gain a thorough grasp of the topic, taking however much time is necessary to do so, you may benefit from carrying out the same procedure with each chapter, as follows:

1. Read the chapter as fast as you can, and preferably at one sitting. As you do this, bear in mind any advice given in the *Points to Consider* section.
2. Study the flow diagram at the end of the chapter, ensuring that you understand the general 'shape' of what you have just read.
3. Read the *Working on ...* section and decide what further work you need to do on the chapter. In particularly important sections of the book, this is likely to involve reading the chapter a second time and stopping at each heading and sub-heading to think about (and probably to write a summary of) what you have just read.
4. Attempt the *Source-based questions* section. It will sometimes be sufficient to think through your answers, but additional understanding will often be gained by forcing yourself to write them down.

When you have finished the main chapters of the book, study the 'Further Reading' section and decide what additional reading (if any) you will do on the topic.

This book has been designed to help make your studies both enjoyable and successful. If you can think of ways in which this could have been done more effectively, please contact us. In the meantime, we hope that you will gain greatly from your study of History.

Keith Randell

1 Introduction

POINTS TO CONSIDER

Do not worry if you find this first chapter confusing. It is simply a summary and a preview of what the subsequent chapters cover and explain in detail. If you can, try to get an overview of race relations in the area now known as the United States of America over the last five hundred years. Start to familiarise yourself with the five main racial groups within America upon whom this book concentrates. Note that some groups have several names by which other Americans refer to them.

KEY DATES

Pre-1400 North American continent inhabited by Native Americans.
1500s First white men settled in North America.
1600s White immigrants dispossessed Native Americans, and imported black slaves from Africa.
1783 Britain's former colonies became the United States of America.
1800s Whites continued to dispossess Native Americans.
1900s Large-scale Hispanic and Asian immigration into the United States. African Americans campaigned for greater equality.

1 America's Racial Groups

> **KEY ISSUE** Who and what is this book about?

All residents of the area now known as the United States of America are referred to as Americans throughout this book. Americans have used colour and/or place of origin to try to distinguish between different racial groups in America. This book deals with the history of the interrelationship between the following racial groups: white Americans, African Americans, Native Americans, Hispanic Americans and Asian Americans.

Most American whites have European/Mediterranean ancestry. For example, there are Americans of British descent, German Americans, Italian Americans, Irish Americans and Jewish Americans. Black Americans are descended from slaves imported from Africa, or from African/Caribbean emigrants. Hispanic Americans are Spanish speaking, but few are of relatively pure Spanish (white European) ancestry. Most Hispanics are a mixture of the African American and Native American races. Previously known as 'Indians', Native

Americans are the descendants of the earliest inhabitants of North America. The Asian American group includes Chinese Americans, Japanese Americans, and those from the Indian subcontinent and Southeast Asia.

This book explains how these groups became 'Americans'. From the fifteenth century onwards, dynamic and expansionist representatives of the white continent of Europe began extending their influence over continents inhabited by races with different skin colours and different cultures, who were generally at earlier stages of economic, technological and political development than Europeans. The Europeanisation of the North American continent had a dramatic impact upon both the native inhabitants, who were dispossessed by the Europeans, and upon the inhabitants of the African continent whom the whites imported into North America as slaves. Whites of British ancestry dominated the new nation that was established in 1783 as the United States of America. During the nineteenth century increased numbers of whites from eastern and southern Europe arrived in America. These were soon assimilated as part of the dominant white group. Whites controlled the legal, social and economic status of blacks and Native Americans, and were wary of allowing non-white racial groups to enter America. East Asians were the first racial group to be legally excluded from America, by the 1882 Chinese Exclusion Act.

Slowly the black minority grew more assertive, culminating in a mid-twentieth century campaign for political, legal, social and economic equality. At the same time, the later twentieth century United States saw an influx of immigrants from Asia and from nearby Spanish speaking areas. The latter spoke Spanish because of Spanish conquest and colonisation. Some Hispanics pre-dated north European settlers in America, while others were nineteenth and twentieth century immigrants from other parts of the Americas.

During the second half of the twentieth century the numbers of racial minorities in the United States rose dramatically due to the relaxation of immigration restrictions and natural population increase. Between 1970 and 1990, non-whites grew from one eighth to one-quarter of America's population. By 1990, African Americans constituted 12%, Hispanics 9%, Asians 3%, and Native Americans 1% of America's population. It is estimated that by the year 2050, non-whites will constitute around half of America's population.

2 Race Relations

KEY ISSUE Why have there been racial tensions?

The Jewish writer Israel Zangwill (1864–1926) first spoke of an

American 'melting pot', in which nationalities and racial groups fused into one. However, racial awareness persisted, resulting in tension. There were frequent ethnic antagonisms, even amongst the white majority. Most famously, mid-nineteenth century New England houses and places of employment frequently displayed signs that said, 'NO IRISH WANTED'. There has also been racial hostility between whites and non-whites, and between different non-white groups. In the 1992 African American riots in Los Angeles, for example, black rioters targeted over three thousand Asian-owned businesses.

Why have the races within America frequently failed to get along? Sadly, the answer seems to be 'human nature'. Before the arrival of white men, Native American tribes warred amongst themselves. Throughout history, people have been hostile towards those from another culture/country/race. The Europeans who conquered the North American continent from the sixteenth century to the nineteenth century, generally assumed that they were superior to the Native Americans. Why? Like many other religions, Christianity encouraged a sense of unique religious rectitude, a corollary of which was that non-Christians had 'got it wrong' and were therefore inferior. When Europeans found the Native Americans to be technologically less advanced, particularly in armaments, that technological superiority seemed to confirm cultural and racial superiority. As the Europeans wanted to acquire Native American land, their sense of superiority was a necessary part of the moral justification for conquest. Other cultures were simply not valued. Future American President Theodore Roosevelt declared in 1889 that it was irrational and immoral to keep 'two-thirds of a splendid continent as a hunting preserve for squalid savages'.

Some Spanish immigrants wanted to 'serve God' by converting the heathen Native American population, and other immigrants had a patriotic desire to gain glory and prestige. However, the majority of the individuals who peopled the North American continent from the fifteenth century to the twentieth century were motivated primarily by the desire for personal improvement. While some sought political freedom, the vast majority sought 'to get rich'. Anyone who got in their way was a threat. Thus a main and continuing source of racial hostility was economic antagonism, accentuated by cultural and physical differences which made the antagonism seem even more threatening.

Most white Americans have always felt superior to, yet threatened by, other racial groups. When the non-white minorities became increasingly assertive, whites became extremely anxious. This book concentrates upon the history of the relations between the white and the non-white races in the twentieth century. It is a history of frequently uneasy coexistence and occasional violence. Some ethnic groups have quietly accepted discrimination, and retreated into their own community, as with Chinese Americans. Of the different ethnic groups in the United States who have been most discriminated against, African Americans have protested most, which is why this book concentrates upon them. Less assertive minorities are also studied, and comparisons are drawn with African Americans.

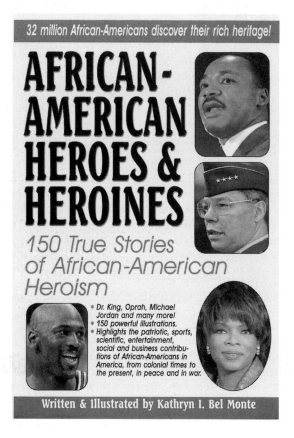

This is the front cover of a book published in the United States in 1998. What do you suppose was the author's purpose in writing it? What does it tell us about African Americans today?

Summary Diagram

Simplified categories of American groups	Other terms for them	Relations with other races
Native Americans	'the red man' Indians	Dispossessed by whites from the 16th–19th century
White Americans	Anglos (sub-groups include Irish Americans, Italian Americans, etc.)	Treated other races as inferior
African Americans	Negroes blacks Afro-Americans	Enslaved by whites until mid 19th century. Still suffered discrimination in the 20th century
Hispanic Americans	Chicanos Latinos Mexican Americans	Tensions with blacks and whites in the 20th century
Asian Americans	Sub-groups include Chinese Americans, Japanese Americans	Tensions with whites (particularly in the late 19th and early 20th centuries) and blacks (particularly in the later 20th century)

Working on Chapter 1

Do not worry if you have found this introductory chapter intimidating. You can always re-read it after you have looked at the following chapters. You might find it useful to construct (now or later) your own date list and/or diagram with boxes to try to clarify your overview of the different races, their arrival in America, and their relationship with each other.

2 The Development of Racial Problems in America, c.1600–1900

POINTS TO CONSIDER

In order to understand twentieth century American race relations, you need to have a basic understanding of what happened before 1900. You need to think about why/whether racial problems were inevitable, and whether the solutions suggested were workable. You need to consider the impact of the Civil War and Reconstruction on the relations between blacks and whites.

KEY DATES

1600s	First Europeans settled in North America.
1619	First black Africans sold to British settlers.
1787	Constitution of the new United States drawn up.
1800s	Whites moved Westward and took Indian lands.
1822	Liberia founded.
1831	Nat Turner's slave revolt.
1857	Supreme Court denied black citizenship (Dred Scott case).
1861–5	Civil War between Southern slave states and Northern states.
1865	South's reconstruction began. 13th Amendment abolished slavery.
1868	14th Amendment said blacks were citizens and authorised federal government intervention if any state abridged citizens' rights.
1870	15th Amendment said vote was not to be denied on account of race.
1875	Civil Rights Act aimed to prevent discrimination in public places, but had little impact in the South.
1880	Most Indians on reservations. Indian children 'civilised' in federal boarding schools.
1890s	Southern states disqualified black voters. Supreme Court (PLESSY v. FERGUSON) approved 'Jim Crow' segregation laws. Frequent lynchings. Many blacks migrated to the North.

1 The Origins of American Racial Problems

FACTUAL ISSUES How did America become multi-racial and why did racial tensions arise?

MORAL ISSUES Who would you blame (and why) for the racial tensions?

a) Discovery, Exploration, and Indians

Before the arrival of white European explorers in the fifteenth century, several million native peoples inhabited North America. Europeans described them as red-skinned and called them 'Indians'. Hence Native Americans were known for a long time as 'Red Indians'.

There are indications that racial tension between white and 'red' was not inevitable. One European explorer expressed amazement at the natives' generosity in the early sixteenth century:

> 1 The greatest token of friendship which they show you is that they give
> you their wives and daughters; and when a father or a mother brings
> you the daughter, although she be a virgin, and you sleep with her, they
> esteem themselves highly honoured; and in this way they practise the
> 5 full extreme of hospitality.[1]

However, relations soon deteriorated, for two main reasons. Firstly, the Europeans' attitude to the Indians was condescending. Europeans thought that all cultures that were different to their own were inferior. For example, seventeenth century English settlers on the East coast of North America thought non-Christian Indians were Satan's agents and responsible for evil, such as the tempting of white women settlers into excessive 'cutting, curling and immodest laying out of their hair'! Secondly, both races wanted possession of the land. Whites felt entitled to take Indian lands without giving any recompense. Tension developed into outright hostility. In 1622 the Indians attacked the English in Virginia and killed one third of the white population, after which the English had few qualms about wiping out any tribes who got in their way. Some Indians were enslaved. For example, there were 1400 Indian slaves in the South Carolina colony in 1708. White immigration had led to cultural and economic clashes with the native population. Racial tension had been introduced to North America.

b) The Introduction of Black People and Slavery

In the early seventeenth century, the Southern colony of Virginia had a persistent labour problem. Therefore, European merchants began to sell black Africans to the English in Virginia. By 1660, slavery was both common and legal. Vast quantities of blacks were easily acquired from Africa, where some African tribal leaders were willing to sell blacks from other tribes to white slave traders. Why did the English consider it acceptable to use blacks as slaves? The Africans had a different, non-Christian culture and were therefore perceived as uncivilised heathens. They looked very different from Europeans and so it seemed acceptable to treat them differently. There was work that needed to be done and too few white men to do it. Slaves could provide cheap and plentiful labour. The expansion of the profitable and labour-intensive tobacco industry in the Southern colonies led to ever-increasing demand for imported African slave labour. All these factors made slavery seem acceptable.

By 1776 British North America contained 2,500,000 people, one fifth of whom were black slaves. There were occasional armed rebellions, as when New York City slaves attacked their white oppressors in 1712. Such unsuccessful revolts demonstrated black resentment and powerlessness. White belief in white supremacy and the overriding importance of white economic needs had led to the development of more racial tension.

c) The Constitution and Race Relations

In 1776 the white American colonists demanded freedom from British rule in their Declaration of Independence. However, few slave owners recognised the contradiction between the ideas of freedom and the fact of slavery.

In 1783 the British government recognised American independence. The Americans had to establish their own form of government for the 13 ex-colonies, now to be called states. Delegates from the states discussed a new constitution. The issue of black slaves was debated. The crucial question was: did a black slave deserve political representation like other (white) human beings or was he merely a piece of property? The Southern states wanted their black slaves to count as human beings for purposes of representation, so that although the slaves could not vote, the South would nevertheless have the maximum number of representatives in Congress (America's Parliament). However, Southerners did not want their slaves to count as human beings if that meant having to pay more taxes. Representatives from the Northern states enjoyed watching Southerners adjusting the status of blacks (human beings or property) according to their needs, and sarcastically asked whether Northerners should have representation for their cattle. The resulting Three-Fifths Compromise settled the issue: five slaves were to equal three free persons for purposes of taxation and legislative representation in Congress. The new American Constitution thus enshrined the inferiority of black slaves. The Constitution also guaranteed the continuation of the slave trade until 1808. The Constitution gave each state government control over the make-up of the electorate and ensured that only privileged white males could vote. The Constitution made no provision for Indians, who were classified as 'foreign nations'. Thus within the context of the new American nation, those whose skin was not white were in many respects non-people. The Constitution of the new nation set out to protect the rights, liberties and freedom of white men, while demonstrating how whites felt about non-whites.

d) Early Reactions to Racism and Slavery

The unequal treatment of non-whites was frequently and blindly over-looked by the Founding Fathers of the new nation. John Jay, for example, wrote that,

Providence has been pleased to give this one connected country to one united people, a people descended from the same ancestors, speaking the same language, professing the same religion, attached to the same principles of government, very similar in their manners and customs.[2]

Another Founding Father, Thomas Jefferson, had been influential in the production of the ringing declaration of 1776 that 'all men are created equal'. However, he said that Americans would be 'obliged' to drive the 'backward' Indians into the mountains like 'beasts of the forests'. The Indians did not farm nor value private property like whites; therefore it was unreasonable that they should retain so much land. On the other hand, Jefferson was hopeful that Indians might eventually blend into and adopt white American 'civilisation'. He was ambivalent about blacks and slavery. He never publicly admitted his affection for his slave and long-standing mistress, nor did he publicly acknowledge their children, only freeing them in his will. He said that he despised slavery and once spoke of freeing his slaves but never did. He said it was difficult to decide whether blacks were inferior to whites or simply made so by the 'peculiar institution' of slavery. Rather conveniently for a slave owner, he said that freeing those brought up in slavery would be like abandoning children.

Many lacked Jefferson's doubts and came down squarely for or against slavery. There were societies advocating the abolition of slavery throughout the new United States, and slavery had been abolished in most Northern states by the early nineteenth century. However, there were few abolitionists in the Southern United States. Why? Wealthy Southerners thought that the profitability of the Southern plantation economy depended upon slave labour. White Southerners who did not own slaves feared that freed slaves would be (cheaper) rivals in the labour market. Rich and poor white Southerners were frightened by the potential hostility of free blacks. One of the most important reasons for the continuation of slavery was that for most white Southerners it served as an effective solution to what they considered would be an intolerable racial problem. The Northern United States was accustomed to greater ethnic diversity: in 1860 one in six Northerners was foreign-born. By contrast, only one in thirty Southerners were born outside the United States. Therefore, white Southerners were more fearful of the dilution of their stock. Over 90% of American blacks lived in the South and their freedom from slavery threatened white supremacy and racial purity in a way that white Northerners could not imagine. After all, slaves outnumbered whites in South Carolina and Mississippi.

Slavery was thus one of several means of race control used by nineteenth century Americans. Was it successful? Not surprisingly, enslavement increased black antagonism. Escape, simulated illness, self-inflicted injury, broken tools, deliberate accidents and deliberate ignorance, and the occasional rebellion demonstrated black discontent. In 1831 an educated and articulate slave called Nat Turner led about 70 other slaves in a slave revolt in which 55 whites (mainly women and children) were killed.

Southerners felt increasingly beleaguered and therefore sought new justifications for slavery. The 'necessary evil' argument was replaced by the 'positive good' argument. This gave Southerners more reasons to maintain slavery. The 'positive good' argument claimed that blacks were happy-go-lucky, lazy, ignorant, and inferior to whites. This made slavery desirable, it was argued. How could this inferior race survive, if not worked, fed and clothed by caring white slave owners?

The introduction and maintenance of slavery in America had led to what seemed like an insoluble problem.

HOW WERE SLAVES TREATED?

Inevitably, the white race's position of unnatural domination led to varying degrees of unhappiness for the black slaves. Most slaves lacked freedom of choice over movement, work, family life, and culture. Some whites did not overwork the slaves, and allowed them to eat well, to have a stable family life, to attend religious meetings, and to learn to read and write. Some were exceptionally cruel. A drunk Kentucky man dismembered his slave and threw him bit by bit into the fire.

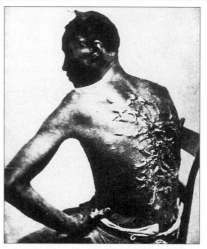

The scarred back of a Louisiana slave who had been beaten by his owner.

Whippings were common. Occasionally, slaves retaliated. A beaten Kentucky slave strangled her mistress.

White women and black men rarely had a sexual relationship. However, as a result of relationships between white men and black female slaves, there were 411,000 mulatto slaves, out of a total slave population of 3.9 million, by 1860. The figure might have been higher, as many mulattos passed as whites.

2 Suggested Solutions

> **KEY ISSUES** What were the suggested solutions to race relations' problems? Were any of them feasible?

a) Indians – Military, Legal, Educational and Segregationist Solutions

Whites had several methods for dealing with the 'Indian problem'. The white man used his superior technology and numbers to gain land militarily from the Indians.

In 1763, a white general thought infecting the Indians with smallpox might be easier than conventional warfare. Blankets and handkerchiefs from a smallpox hospital were distributed amongst the Delaware Indians. Whether that early attempt at biological warfare was responsible for the smallpox epidemic that soon raged amongst the Delawares is difficult to determine. Many whites favoured 'ethnic cleansing'. General Carleton said Indian men should be 'slain whenever and wherever they can be found.' In 1868, General Philip Sheridan epitomised the attitude of many Western whites:

> The more [Indians] we can kill this year, the less will have to be killed next year. For the more I see of the Indian, the more convinced I am that all will have to be killed or maintained as paupers.[3]

The historian William T. Hagan[4] has likened the worst instances of the enforced removal of tribes from their ancestral lands to the Nazi treatment of subject peoples in World War Two. Between 1829 and 1866 the Winnebago tribe was moved six times. Some Indian leaders felt death in battle preferable to a living death under white rule. Thus Indians contemplated suicide and whites contemplated genocide as solutions to the clash between the red and white races. In practice, white treatment of the Indians approached genocide. Before the whites arrived in America, there were several million Indians; by 1900, there were a quarter of a million.

Diplomacy was another way of handling the Indians. The Indians signed many treaties with white Americans. Treaties were often synonymous with trickery. In 1809, for example, after an American official 'mellowed' several Indian chiefs with alcohol, the chiefs signed away three million acres of land in Indiana. The treaties supposedly guaranteed that the Indians retained some lands but whites broke the treaties when it suited them. White Americans found it easy to give ideological justification for their territorial expansion and their illegal breaking of treaties with Indians. A governor of Georgia said,

> treaties were expedients by which ignorant, intractable and savage

people were induced without bloodshed to yield up what civilised people had a right to possess.[5]

One government official believed

1 The idea that a handful of wild, half naked, thieving, plundering, murdering savages should be dignified with the sovereign attributes of nations, enter into solemn treaties, and claim a country 500 miles wide by 1000 miles long as theirs ... because they hunted buffalo and ante-
5 lope over it ... is unsuited to the intelligence and justice of this age, or the natural rights of mankind.[6]

In 1887 the Dawes Act allotted reservation land to Indians. The act aimed to eliminate the concept of tribal lands and convert Indians to the ownership of private property, which whites considered essential to civilisation and progress. The act ensured that there was ample reservation land left for redistribution to whites. Whites frequently obtained allotted lands cheaply from uncomprehending Indians. Between 1887 and 1934, Indians lost 86 million out of a total of 138 million acres. Most of that which remained was undesirable semidesert.

Obtaining Indian land was thus effected by military and dubiously legal methods. However, the racial problem remained. Sympathetic whites thought the Indians' best chance of survival lay in 'Americanisation' – the rejection of traditional Indian culture and the assimilation of white culture. This integrationist solution climaxed in the 1880s when Indian children were taken away from parental influence and 'civilised' in federal-funded boarding schools. The policy did not work. Whites and Indians both refused to accept 'educated' Indians. The Indian children often suffered greatly. For example, the federal government ordered that all male Indians in the schools should cut their hair, because long hair represented resistance to civilisation. On some reservations, Indian boys had to be shackled for their hair cutting, because they believed that long hair had supernatural significance for rain ceremonies and that they were doomed if their hair fell into enemy hands. Sun Elk, a Pueblo Indian, remembered:

We all wore white man's clothes and ate white man's food and went to white man's churches and spoke white man's talk. And so after a while we also began to say Indians were bad. We laughed at our own people and their blankets and cooking pots and sacred societies and dances.[7]

A Chippewa student described the impact of her boarding school education:

1 Did I want to be an Indian? After looking at the pictures of the Indians on the warpath – fighting, scalping women and children, and Oh! Such

ugly faces. No! Indians are mean people – I'm glad I'm not an Indian, I
thought.... Gone were the vivid pictures of my parents, sisters and
5 brothers. Only a blurred vision of what used to be. Desperately, I tried
to cling to the faded past which was slowly being erased from my mind.[8]

Sun Elk recalled the result of his schooling experience:

1 It was a warm summer evening when I got off the train at Taos station.
The first Indian I met, I asked him to run out to the pueblo and tell my
family I was home. The Indian couldn't speak English, and I had forgot-
ten all my Pueblo language.... Next morning ... two war chiefs ... came
5 into my father's house. They ... said to my father, 'Your son who calls
himself Rafael has lived with the white men. He has been far away....
He has not ... learned the things that Indian boys should learn. He has
no hair.... He cannot even speak our language. He is not one of us.'[9]

The later nineteenth century practice of putting Indians on reservations constituted a policy of geographical racial separation. By the
1880s most Indians had been settled on reservations. These were
always the inhospitable areas that white men did not want.
Sometimes, as in the Black Hills of Dakota gold rush, whites changed
their minds about the value of reservation land. The Indians then had
to move to a reservation elsewhere. One Indian chief said,

Since the Great Father [the American President] promised that we
should never be removed, we have been moved five times.... Why
does not the Great Father put his red children on wheels, so he can
move them as he will?[10]

So, after three centuries of struggle, white domination over the
Indians was total. By 1900, whites considered the Indian problem
solved.

b) Hispanics – the 'No More Imperialism' Solution

The white American expansion over large parts of the North
American continent necessitated not only the dispossession of
Indians, but also the acquisition of Western territories such as
California, New Mexico and Texas, which had belonged to Mexico.
By the mid-nineteenth century whites outnumbered Hispanics in
the American West. Light-skinned members of the Hispanic elite
were accepted into the dominant American elite, but darker
skinned Hispanics were kept socially, politically and economically
inferior.

Some Americans favoured the acquisition of Mexico itself, but the
Mexican people were primarily of Native American ethnicity and so a
leading Southerner objected:

To incorporate Mexico would be the very first instance ... of incorpo-
rating an Indian race; for more than half of the Mexicans are Indians, and

the other is composed chiefly of mixed tribes. I protest against such a union as that! Ours, sir, is the government of a white race.[11]

Thus an occasional solution to the race problem suggested by white Americans was to desist from further imperialism.

c) Chinese – the 'Stop Immigration' Solution

Immigrants flocked to the increasingly prosperous United States. Up to the mid-nineteenth century most immigrants were of white, Protestant, north European stock, but soon there was greater diversity. Chinese immigrants were particularly unpopular. Chinese men were first attracted by the discovery of gold in California in the 1840s. They were encouraged to come to the West as cheap labour for the transcontinental railroad building in the 1860s. By 1870 there were nearly 100,000 Chinese in California, where they constituted about 10% of the population. There was racism from the start. Chinese workers were frequently driven out by mob violence. Whites considered it a joke to cut off the pigtail without which a Chinese male would be unacceptable in China. White Californians felt threatened by Chinese willingness to work for lower wages, culminating in anti-Chinese riots in Chinatown in San Francisco in 1877. As a result, Congress passed the Chinese Exclusion Act (1882) prohibiting Chinese immigration.

d) Blacks – Repatriation and Emigration Solutions

One suggested solution to the 'black problem' was the repatriation of freed slaves. The American Colonisation Society aimed to compensate slave-owners and send their slaves back to Africa. Under this programme, about 12,000 blacks returned to Africa to the new Republic of Liberia after its foundation in 1822. However, Liberia was not a popular solution. Black people felt that North America was their home. They did not want to leave their home. They simply wanted to get better treatment there. Colonisation thus became unfashionable after 1830 but it revived in the 1850s when some white politicians and blacks argued that black freedom necessitated departure from America. Some black separatists emigrated to Haiti to escape America and racism. Others, subsidised by the federal government, went to live in Panama and the Caribbean islands, but these black migrations were never very popular among the majority of black Americans. Clearly, attempts to get rid of blacks were an unworkable solution.

e) Segregation and Victimisation of Northern Blacks

What was the situation of Northern blacks before the Civil War? In

1860 there were around a quarter of a million free blacks in the North. They were not treated as equals. Although the Democratic Party talked much of increasing political democracy, enthusiasm for widening of the franchise did not extend to women, Indians or blacks. One opponent of black suffrage said blacks were 'peculiar' people who were 'incapable' of exercising the vote 'with any sort of discretion, prudence or independence. They have no just conceptions of civil liberty'.[12]

Before the Civil War, New York state disqualified 30,000 free black residents from voting. In the 1850s Northern states refused to allow free blacks entry. 'It is certainly the wish of every patriot,' said a leading Republican, that 'our union should be homogeneous in race and of our own blood.' During economic recessions, black workers were the first to lose their jobs. White mobs frequently attacked black workers for accepting lower wages. In Northern towns, black Americans were excluded from white institutions and public facilities, and were unofficially segregated in schools, churches and housing. When a white Quaker teacher admitted a black girl to her Connecticut school, white patrons boycotted it and eventually got the teacher arrested on trumped up charges. The Quakers of Pennsylvania welcomed blacks to their religious services but even they maintained segregated burial places. Thus Northern solutions to the problem of black and white relations included segregation and discrimination. There were Northern whites who favoured integration, and many believed the first step toward that to be the abolition of slavery. Nevertheless many white abolitionists looked down on blacks and did not envisage equality or integration. In the 1830s the French visitor De Tocqueville thought that racism was stronger in the North than the South! Segregation was often the most appealing solution to blacks. They could maintain their cultural identity in their own churches, and avoid white officialdom while living in segregated areas. Proximity seemed to exacerbate racial tension: a high proportion of race riots occurred in areas containing a large black minority.

Several answers to America's race problems were thus suggested in the nineteenth century: controlled emigration and immigration, social and/or geographical segregation, integration and the continuation of slavery. Even the 75% of white Southerners who did not own slaves agreed that slavery was an effective method of social control. Disagreements over this Southern solution to the race problem were to contribute to the Civil War between the Northern and Southern states.

3 Slavery and the Civil War

KEY ISSUES How important were slavery and racism in causing the Civil War? Were Northerners and Southerners equally racist?

a) Events Leading up to the Civil War

From the early nineteenth century, as white Americans moved Westward, new land was acquired and admitted to statehood. The question of whether to allow slavery therein was hotly debated. Many Northerners were opposed to the extension of slavery. Some had been turned against slavery by abolitionists. Some objected to the presence of non-whites in new territories to which Northerners might want to migrate. Some felt cheap slave labour would make it harder for whites to gain employment. Some feared that more slave states would increase the political power of the South within the union.

In 1819 Missouri applied for admission as a state of the union. Northerners proposed excluding slavery from Missouri. Southerners were furious. Northerners seemed to be claiming moral superiority and to be sthreatening to decrease Southern influence in Congress if no new state was allowed in with slavery. The answer was the Missouri Compromise (1820): Congress allowed Missouri in as a slave state but balanced it with the admission of Maine as a free state. The continuing acquisition of new territories ensured that North/South tension would not go away. In the Dred Scott case (1857) the Supreme Court said that blacks were not US citizens and that Congress lacked the constitutional authority to exclude slavery from new states.

North/South tension was increased by extremism on both sides. The Republican Party opposed the extension of slavery. To Southerners, the election of the Republican President Abraham Lincoln seemed threatening. In 1860–1, the Southern states left the Union and formed the Confederate States of America. The Confederacy's constitution was modelled on the American Constitution and guaranteed slavery, while rejecting the slave trade.

b) Was the Civil War a War to End Slavery?

Although the extension of slavery was possibly the major cause of the Civil War (1861–5), that war was not fought to end slavery. Most Northerners thought they were fighting to save the Union (of the United States) and not to free Southern slaves. Northerners feared that freed slaves would migrate to the North and flood the labour market and cause racial tension. Lincoln was no exception to the norm. While opposing the extension of slavery to new states, President Lincoln declared himself willing to protect the institution where it existed. He did not want to alienate his supporters in slave states. 'We did not go to war to put down slavery', he told Congress in December 1861. In September 1862, however, for primarily military reasons, Lincoln issued his Emancipation Proclamation. This proclamation aimed to hamper the Southern war effort. It freed around 4 million slaves in the Confederacy but not in loyal states wherein slavery existed. (Slavery was finally ended throughout the US after

Lincoln's death in 1865.) While Lincoln declared slavery 'the greatest wrong inflicted on any people', he had nevertheless been willing to countenance its continued existence in the South, and he had hoped for colonisation and the departure of all blacks. 'There must be the position of superior and inferior,' he said, and he was 'in favour of having the superior position assigned to the white race.' He told a black audience that in America,

> not a single man of your race is made the equal of a single man of ours
> ... I cannot alter it if I would. It is a fact, about which we all think and
> feel alike, I and you ... it is better for us to be separated.[13]

For Lincoln then, as for most Northerners, the Civil War was not a war for racial equality but for preservation of the Union. Even so, for the electorate in the 1864 presidential election, one of the Democrats' most effective anti-Lincoln criticisms was that he was a 'Negro lover' plotting 'miscegenation' (co-mingling of the black and white races). Lincoln's views were slightly modified during the war. Initially he had not wanted Indians and blacks in the Union army. However, he was impressed by the performance of black soldiers, and contemplated giving the vote to 'the very intelligent' and most gallant.

There was considerable hostility toward blacks in the North in the Civil War. Northern race relations were poor before the war (see pages 14–15). Now some newspapers claimed Lincoln had got America into a Civil War to help undeserving blacks. When Southern slaves had first rushed to join Union forces the latter were highly suspicious. White conservatives in the North disliked the idea of arming Northern blacks whom they considered inferior and unreliable. However, by 1865, 10% of Union troops were black. They came from the South as well as the North. Nearly half a million Southern slaves had joined the Union army. Black troops, although brave and enthusiastic, were given the worst and most dangerous tasks. They were usually paid less than whites. However, the *New York Times* felt there had been a 'prodigious revolution' in the public mind: in 1863 a New York Irish mob had attacked blacks in protest against the idea of black soldiers, but in 1865 black soldiers were given an affectionate farewell parade in the same city. The *New York Times* thought that signalled 'a new epoch'. The new epoch, however, did not mean that blacks attained equality. Although three amendments to the Constitution from 1865–70 gave rights of citizenship to the ex-slaves, real equality was far away.

4 Reconstruction and Segregation

KEY ISSUES Did the Civil War and Reconstruction produce a new and better world for Southern blacks? Were blacks 'equal' in the nineteenth century North?

a) The Post-war South

The post-war South experienced great changes. After the Civil War, 700,000 blacks were registered to vote in the South, compared to 600,000 eligible whites. In the Civil War era, radical Republicans had advocated equal voting rights for blacks, so Lincoln's Republican Party now acquired the black votes. The Fourteenth Amendment to the Constitution (1868) granted citizenship to all former male slaves. It gave equality before the law to all. The Fifteenth Amendment (1870) said the right to vote 'shall not be denied ... on account of race, color, or previous condition of servitude.'

Although there were more black Republicans, white Republicans dominated the Southern states during Reconstruction. Scores of Republican blacks were elected to local and state office, but there was no Southern black governor during Reconstruction, nor any black majority in any state senate. Only South Carolina (65% black) had a black majority in the lower house. There were only two black US senators, both from Mississippi (over 50% black). One of them was shot by whites in a tavern. When he begged them to let him die out in the fresh air, they took him out to the street and pumped him full of 30 extra bullets. Most black politicians simply followed the white lead. White Republicans watched the gradual re-incorporation of Southern whites into the political process with sympathy.

Although slavery had gone, Southerners still believed in the arguments that had justified it. Southern whites who were inevitably frightened and resentful of the supposedly racially inferior blacks distorted the reality of the Reconstruction era. It suited Southern whites to depict Reconstruction as an era of black rule, rape, murder and arson. They made this an excuse to call for the disfranchisement of blacks. They used violence to stop blacks voting. In the 1890s the Southern state legislatures introduced income and literacy qualifications for voting, which penalised more blacks than whites. Illiterate whites were often allowed to vote through notorious 'grandfather clauses', by which a man could vote if it were proved that an ancestor had voted before Reconstruction! Some whites claimed that blacks were immature, irrational, open to corruption, and therefore unfit to possess voting rights. One Mississippi man said that even an educated black like Booker T. Washington (see pages 25–34) was no more fit to vote than 'the coconut-headed, chocolate-coloured, typical little coon' who 'blacks my shoes' and was not 'fit to perform the supreme function of citizenship'. White Southern registrars even connived at the disqualification of literate blacks by manipulating the literacy test. Reconstruction thus failed to bring lasting political gains for blacks.

Reconstruction failed to bring great economic gains to blacks. Freed black slaves had acquired freedom of movement but because they lacked wealth most remained in the South and farmed. Most

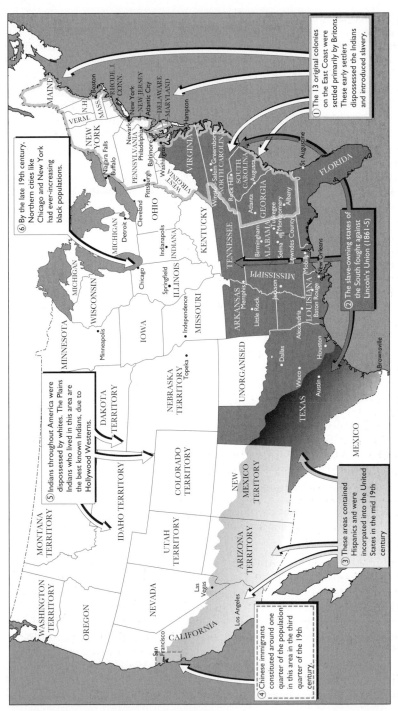

① The 13 original colonies on the East Coast were settled primarily by Britons. These early settlers dispossessed the Indians and introduced slavery.

② The slave-owning states of the South fought against Lincoln's Union (1861–5)

③ These areas contained Hispanics and were incorporated into the United States in the mid 19th century

④ Chinese immigrants constituted around one quarter of the population in this area in the third quarter of the 19th century.

⑤ Indians throughout America were dispossessed by whites. The Plains Indians who lived in this area are the best known Indians, due to Hollywood Westerns.

⑥ By the late 19th century, Northern cities like Chicago and New York had ever-increasing black populations.

Race relations in the United States in the mid-nineteenth century.

remained in the poverty trap. They could only work as tenant farmers for the white elite in a South which was economically far behind the North. The lack of economic power kept black progress slow.

Reconstruction brought some social gains for blacks. It gave some blacks the confidence and opportunity to build and benefit from their own institutions. Black churches and the federal Freedmen's Bureau (1865–72) made education more widely available to blacks, and a few black political leaders, businessmen, teachers, lawyers and doctors emerged. Some of the institutions founded during Reconstruction, including colleges of higher education like Howard and Fisk, provided the kind of race leaders necessary for the civil rights movement of the mid twentieth century. Black churches became immensely popular and influential, although naturally they served to perpetuate the social divisions between blacks and whites.

Despite the lack of real black advancement after the Civil War, whites remained fearful. A white Georgian said:

> There is absolutely no place in this land for the arrogant, aggressive, school-spoilt African American who wants to live without manual labour. Yes Sir! We know Sambo, and we like him first rate, in his place. And he must stay there, too.[14]

A group of Southern politicians created an anti-Negro crusading group in the 1890s. They depicted blacks as characterised by 'barbarism, voodooism, human sacrifice', and 'contaminated by venereal disease'. Some white politicians advocated deportation, others wanted

> to emasculate [castrate] the entire Negro race and thus prevent any further danger from them, and the horrors of their crossing continually with the Anglo-Saxon stock.[15]

A Georgia congressman said in 1908,

> The utter extermination of a race of people is inexpressibly sad, yet if its existence endangers the welfare of mankind, it is fitting that it should be swept away.[16]

The powers given to individual states under the Constitution facilitated the introduction of laws that discriminated against blacks. Individual states controlled not only voting but education, transport, and law enforcement. The segregation of schools, housing and public facilities spread quickly after 1865. Between 1881 and 1915 many Southern states passed laws which insisted upon the separation of white from black in trains, streetcars, stations, theatres, churches, parks, schools, restaurants, and cemeteries. Whites were not to use black prostitutes. Textbooks for use in white schools were not to be stored in the same place as those for black schools. Blacks and whites were forbidden to play checkers [draughts] together. No doubt many blacks felt more comfortable being thus segregated.

White violence against blacks was endemic in the post-war South. Unlawful hangings (lynchings) of blacks by paramilitary white supremacist groups such as the Ku Klux Klan were common. Between 1885 and 1917, 2734 blacks were lynched in the United States. Those responsible for the lynchings were never brought to justice, indicating widespread support for their actions. Blacks had no legal protection. The Supreme Court did nothing about the so-called (no one knows why) 'Jim Crow' laws that legalised segregation. In 1896 (PLESSY v. FERGUSON) the Supreme Court said separate but equal facilities were not against the Fourteenth Amendment. The Supreme Court did not prevent Southern states spending ten times as much on white schools as on black, nor did it uphold the Fifteenth Amendment, which said blacks should be able to vote. Thus the South ignored the US Constitution with the collusion of the Supreme Court.

After Reconstruction, Southern black Americans had little help from either the federal government or the Supreme Court. They faced hostility from many Southern whites. By 1900, Jim Crow laws had undermined most of the gains from Reconstruction. Defeat in the Civil War and the experience of Reconstruction embittered whites and made racial tensions worse than in the pre-war period. On the other hand, the end of slavery gave blacks more opportunities, and while the Fourteenth and Fifteenth Amendments were usually ignored, they remained part of the Constitution, to be appealed to in later years. A common black saying summed it up: 'We ain't what we ought to be, we ain't what we going to be. But thank God we ain't what we used to be.'

b) Blacks in the North

In the industrialised North, blacks had legal and political equality. However, whites considered blacks competition for jobs and housing, and resented it when black votes affected the outcome of local elections. Businessmen exploited such divisions, frequently using blacks as strikebreakers. Even if a Northern black were better educated and more skilled than a white worker, the latter would get priority in the job market. The rural South offered few economic opportunities to blacks who could only work the land owned by whites, so increasing numbers migrated to the North seeking work. In Chicago there were 15,000 blacks in 1890, and 50,000 by 1915. These unskilled and uneducated Southern blacks were greatly disadvantaged when they came North. In Boston, 12% of first-generation Irish-Americans were white-collar workers, increasing to 24% in the second generation; the figures for blacks were 7% increasing to only 9%. While blacks had been scattered throughout Northern cities in 1880, they were in ghettos that were 90% or more homogeneous after 1900. Although black men usually had low paid labouring jobs and women were in even lower paid domestic service, rents were higher within the restricted boundaries of the black ghetto, than in white neighbourhoods. In 1910 Chicago, a seven-room apartment for working class whites was $25 weekly, for blacks, $37.50.

c) The Situation in 1900

America thus prepared to embark upon the twentieth century with multiple racial problems. A large black minority and small Indian, Hispanic and Chinese minorities were faced with a white majority who feared racial mixing and were convinced of the supremacy of the white race. Anthropologist Joseph Le Conte asserted that,

> modern ethnologists have thoroughly established the fact that in all essential qualities the Negro race seems to be totally incapable of development.[17]

Fearful whites retreated to segregated educational institutions and residential areas, away from those whose skin was black, red or yellow.

Why did non-whites apparently accept this position of inferiority? Blacks had to overcome *de jure* [legal] discrimination in the South, and *de facto* [actual] discrimination in the North. The end of slavery had left Southern blacks with freedom of movement but without material resources. Most blacks were in a poverty trap. Indians were divided amongst themselves, due to tribal rivalries and disagreements as to the wisdom of rejecting their traditional culture in favour of the white man's. Deprived of their traditional lands, Indians were also locked in a poverty trap. Far more than blacks, most Indians lacked both organisation and understanding of the white man's laws and concepts such as private property. However, while the nineteenth century saw the virtually unchallenged domination of whites over other races in America, the twentieth century saw attempts to alter the balance.

References

1 P.N. Carroll and D.W. Noble, *The Free and the Unfree*, Penguin Putnam Inc., 1988, p. 35.
2 Ibid., p. 133.
3 Quoted in Alan Farmer, *Reconstruction and the Results of the American Civil War*, London, p. 134.
4 William T. Hagan, *American Indians*, The University of Chicago Press, 1993,
   p. 87.
5 *Free and Unfree*, p. 172.
6 Ibid., p. 233.
7 Quoted in *500 Nations*, by Alvin M. Josephy, New York, 1994, p. 434.
8 Ibid., p. 434.

9   Ibid., p. 436.
10 Hagan, p. 133.
11 Senator John Calhoun, quoted on p. 175, *The Free and the Unfree.*
12 Ibid., p. 198.
13 Ibid., p. 223.
14 Ibid., p. 253.
15 Ibid., p. 255.
16 Ibid., p. 255.
17 Ibid., p. 253.

Summary Diagram
The Origins and Development of Racial Problems in America, c. 1600–1900

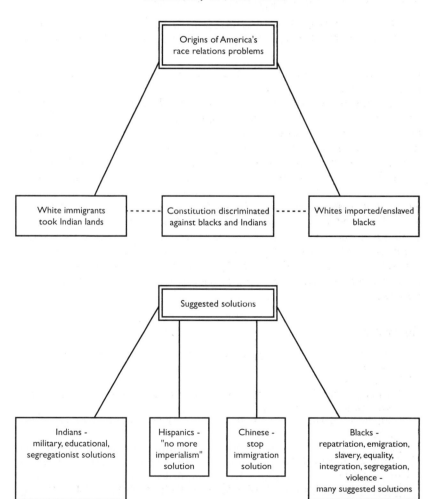

Working on Chapter 2

In order to clarify your thoughts on the origins of American race relations' problems, and suggested solutions to them, you might find it helpful to work through each racial group separately. You could ask the same factual and analytical questions for each group (Indians, blacks, Hispanics, and Asians). For example: When did racial tension start? What caused it? Why did it continue? Who or what bore most responsibility? What solutions were suggested? Were the solutions workable? If not, why not? Does any individual reflect typical contemporary attitudes? What did he say? Had life steadily improved, steadily worsened, or done both at different times, for the racial group before 1900? (You could draw graphs to illustrate this.)

Having attempted answers for these questions for each group, you could then note similarities and differences between the groups' experiences.

Answering structured and essay questions on Chapter 2

In order to help establish the content of this chapter in your mind, you might find it useful to think through possible exam questions on the subject matter, such as these two AS structured questions:

a) How and why was slavery introduced and maintained in North America from the seventeenth century to 1800? (*8 marks*)
b) Explain the differing attitudes of white Americans to blacks during the nineteenth century. (*12 marks*)

When answering (a) watch out for the difference between HOW and WHY. HOW invites you to say WHO, WHAT and WHEN. For example, who/what introduced slavery and ensured its continuation? At each stage of your explanation of how slavery began and continued, give reasons WHY it seemed desirable and appropriate.

Examiners like you to study change over time. Such studies lend themselves to full (A 2) essay questions, for example:

1 How and why did the situation of American blacks change between 1600 and 1900?
2 How and why did the situation of American Indians change between 1600 and 1900?

When answering these questions you again need a factual outline (HOW) and analytical explanations for those facts (WHY). Watch the dates closely, and remember that change does not always mean progression to something better. Sometimes, as with the blacks, things got better, then worse, then slightly better again.

Origins of the Black Civil Rights Movement, 1900–45

3

POINTS TO CONSIDER

By the 1960s, many black Americans were united in a dramatic civil rights campaign. How and to what extent had the years 1900 to 1945 helped to prepare the way? As you read this chapter, think about the contributions of individuals like Booker T. Washington, organisations such as the National Association for the Advancement of Colored People (NAACP), and events such as two world wars and the Depression. Consider which were the most important. Compare the situation of blacks in 1900 and 1945 and decide how much their situation had improved.

KEY DATES

1901	Booker T. Washington dined at White House.
1905	Du Bois established the Niagara Movement (NAACP).
1906	President Theodore Roosevelt criticised black criminality.
1914–18	World War One stimulated great black migration North.
	President Wilson tried to segregate the civil service.
1933	President Franklin Roosevelt's New Deal helped poor blacks.
1937	Anti-lynching bill failed in Senate.
1939–45	World War Two increased black consciousness.
1943	Blacks riots in Harlem, Detroit, and Alabama.
	Roosevelt set up Fair Employment Practices Commission.
1944	Supreme Court declared exclusion of blacks from state primaries unconstitutional.

1 Booker T. Washington and the 'decades of disappointment' (1880–1915)

KEY ISSUES   Were the years 1880–1915 the 'decades of disappointment'? What do Booker T. Washington's life and career reveal about race relations and opportunities for American blacks in those decades? How much did Washington achieve for blacks? Did he pursue the correct strategy for improving life for blacks? Was he just an 'Uncle Tom'? (The Northern abolitionist Harriet Beecher Stowe wrote the book 'Uncle Tom's Cabin' in 1852. Her Uncle Tom character was a slave who deferred to whites. Twentieth century blacks called other blacks 'Uncle Tom' if they seemed too deferential to whites.)

Some historians have described the years between 1880–1915 as the 'decades of disappointment' for blacks.[1] Chapter 2 has shown how much of the promise of the 1860s was not fulfilled. Some blacks saw hope in the career and the achievements of Booker T. Washington, but towards the end of his life others despised and rejected him.

The study of Washington's career and achievements illustrates race relations between 1856 and 1915 and casts light upon two controversies. Were these the 'decades of disappointment' or were race relations and opportunities for blacks improving? Did Washington achieve anything for his people or was he simply an 'Uncle Tom'?

a) Booker T. Washington's Life up to 1895: What Does It Reveal About Race Relations and Opportunities for Blacks?

The first 40 years of Washington's life illuminate the problems and opportunities that faced blacks in the second half of the nineteenth century. As you read the narrative, analyse the material and decide for yourself whether race relations were uniformly bad and to what extent the years after the Civil War were 'decades of disappointment'.

Washington was born into slavery on a Virginia tobacco plantation in 1856. He was brought up in a dirt-floored log cabin without windows or beds. His mother was a black slave. His grey eyes and reddish hair were a legacy from a white father who never admitted that Booker was his son. Washington subsequently said he was fond of his white owners and worried about their safety in the Civil War. His family's rejoicing at the Emancipation Proclamation (see page 16) soon turned into uncertainty about what to do with freedom. They moved to West Virginia, where Washington worked as a salt packer, coal miner and domestic servant. He also managed to obtain some schooling. Washington's ambition was to attend Hampton Institute in Virginia. A group of Northern whites had established Hampton in 1868 in order to teach trades and industry to black men freed after the Civil War. The Virginia state government had given it financial assistance in 1872. With help from his white employer and black friends, Washington set off for Hampton. He was forced to spend the first night of the journey outside a hotel that would not accept black guests. He arrived at Hampton in 1872.

As a result of being born into slavery, Washington had a great deal to learn both intellectually and socially. It took him a long time to work out why his bed was provided with two sheets. Initially, he slept on top of both, then underneath both, then finally got it right by observing the other students. Washington was one of Hampton's youngest students; some were in their forties. Extra help was given to poor students. A white New England philanthropist gave Washington financial assistance and his maths teacher Miss Mackie gave him paid jobs. He was surprised that this well educated white woman from a wealthy family cleaned the school buildings alongside him. Washington returned to West Virginia to teach in 1875. He was saddened when his old white employer died trying to protect blacks in a clash with the white supremacists of the Ku Klux Klan. Hampton asked him to help educate Indians. It was a difficult job. Indians considered blacks inferior for having accepted slavery. Many Indians had themselves owned slaves before Emancipation.

Washington was such a successful teacher that he was offered the post of founder and head of an institute of higher education for blacks in Tuskegee, Alabama. The idea of a black principal was revolutionary. The task was daunting. The Alabama authorities gave Tuskegee Institute minimal funding. Lacking school buildings, Washington had to teach in an abandoned chicken coop with a leaking roof. A student had to hold an umbrella over his head. Nevertheless, the Institute soon had 70 students. Washington employed black teachers. One, Olivia Davidson, later married the widower Washington. Born into slavery, Davidson had lost a brother to the Ku Klux Klan. The wife of President Hayes funded her education at Hampton.

In 1882, Washington purchased an old plantation with donations he had solicited from wealthy Northern whites. Washington led the reluctant students in cleaning up the hen house and stable. He felt the best opportunities for blacks lay in industrial trades, so his curriculum concentrated on practical subjects. Tuskegee taught modern agricultural techniques, trained skilled artisans, and prepared female students to be good housekeepers. Washington's first wife (who was part Indian) taught the female students. Some teachers, students and parents disagreed with Washington's emphasis on the importance of some physical labour for students.

Washington's reputation grew. He was invited to address a prestigious national education conference in Wisconsin (1883). It was the first time that such a conference discussed black and Indian education. Some of the black delegates were turned away from their pre-booked hotel rooms, but when the conference organisers threatened the hotel with a lawsuit they were allowed in. Washington's speech was a plea for racial harmony. However, he was quick to complain in the press when whites threatened some Tuskegee teachers who travelled in a first-class railroad car. Although the Tuskegee teachers had paid for first class tickets, railway officials had forced them to travel some of the way in the far inferior 'Jim Crow' car.

Washington had an increasing number of public-speaking engagements to fulfil. By 1895 he was recognised as America's leading spokesman for black people and their concerns.

b) What Did Booker T. Washington Achieve for Blacks?

Through his work at Tuskegee, Washington helped give several generations of blacks vocational education which increased their self-confidence and economic opportunities. In 1900 he established the National Negro Business League which supported black enterprises. His own struggle for education, and his speeches, books and national fame inspired other blacks to seek education and improvement. It was rarely easy. Washington's daughter graduated from Tuskegee in 1900. She went on to a prestigious Northern women's college, Wellesley. Because of her colour she was forbidden to live on the campus like the other students so she moved to another college.

As the pre-eminent spokesman for blacks, Washington had the responsibility for expressing black concerns. One of his most famous speeches was at the opening of the Atlanta World Fair (1895). Because Atlanta's white leadership wanted to project a new image of enlightened racial harmony, the Fair had a 'Negro Building' to demonstrate black progress at Hampton and Tuskegee. Washington was invited to speak. No black speaker had ever appeared before such an important Southern gathering. The audience included many proud blacks, but also some resentful whites ready to heckle or riot. Contemporary assessments of the quality of his speech and ideas differed. A minority heckled, but Washington's moderate speech (which became known as the 'Atlanta Compromise') did not provoke a riot. He said blacks should not be ashamed of the fact 'that the masses of us are to live by the productions of our hands'. He said it was foolish to agitate for social equality. Equality would come through hard work not force, as no one of economic importance was ever ostracised for long.[2] Northern black militants thought that when Washington sought limited economic opportunity and slow progress toward equality, he sought too little. Other blacks felt that at present limited economic gains were all that they could hope for and were better than nothing. Washington's willingness to accept social segregation was acceptable to many blacks who had little desire to mix with whites. Other blacks felt that any kind of segregation contributed to the perpetuation of racial inequality. Southern white supremacists thought he sought too much for blacks, even though his 'Atlanta Compromise' accepted segregation, and despite the fact that he emphasised whites should not fear blacks:

i As we have proved our loyalty to you in the past, in nursing your children, watching by the sick bed of your mothers and fathers, and often following them with tear-dimmed eyes to their graves, so in the future, in our humble way, we shall stand by you with a devotion that no for-
5 eigner can approach, ready to lay down our lives, if need be, in defence of yours.[3]

Washington's role as black spokesman was not limited to speeches. In the early twentieth century, he began publishing books. The manufacturer of Kodak cameras claimed it was reading Washington's autobiographical *Up From Slavery* that made him donate $10,000 to Tuskegee. The book was artfully written. It was an inspiring story of black achievement. It emphasised racial harmony rather than conflict and gave due credit to any whites who had helped Washington.

In his position as the leading black spokesman honours and opportunities abounded. Washington was the first black to be awarded an honorary Harvard degree (1896). Washington met, impressed and befriended a succession of American presidents, starting with President Cleveland. Cleveland became a patron of Tuskegee Institute. Presidents had to take notice of Washington. He was becoming an international figure. On a European vacation, he was invited to tea with Queen Victoria. In 1896 Washington met President McKinley. He became McKinley's adviser on black affairs. The Southern press was critical of a white president associating closely with Washington, and was particularly hostile when Washington referred to the 'unjust discrimination that law and custom make' against blacks in 'their own country'. As McKinley appointed many blacks to governmental positions, racial tensions increased, and there were race riots across America. In 1901 President Theodore Roosevelt invited Washington to an official dinner at the White House, the first black thus honoured. The visit was greatly criticised in the white Southern press. One writer said that while he honoured Washington, 'no Southern gentlemen could sit at table with him' under any circumstances. Despite the controversy, there was no doubt that Washington's relationships with presidents were raising the black profile and black morale.

Washington's contact with presidents did not always help blacks. Although Theodore Roosevelt paid lip service to the advancement of blacks in government, he cut back the number of black political appointments. In 1904 Washington tried but failed to get Roosevelt's Republican Party to condemn lynching and disfranchisement. Washington and Roosevelt bitterly disagreed about the 'Brownsville riots'. A white man was killed in a shoot-out between blacks and whites outside Fort Brown, Texas (1906). An armed mob from nearby Brownsville marched on the fort demanding that black troops be punished. The black troops denied involvement. Their white officers disbelieved them. The matter was referred to President Roosevelt and raised racial tension nationwide. Whites in Atlanta attacked the city's black business district for five days: ten blacks died, and many fled the city. Despite Washington's pleas, Roosevelt decided to dismiss all the black soldiers at Fort Brown. In a message to Congress in 1906, Roosevelt justified the lynching of blacks as a lesser crime than blacks raping white women, which he claimed to be the cause of the lynchings. As Roosevelt's advisor on black affairs, Washington had read the speech in advance. His failure to get Roosevelt to moderate it demonstrated his impotence. Black militants increasingly regarded Washington as an 'Uncle Tom' who hung around condescending whites who did nothing for him or his people.

In 1908, Washington managed to dissuade President Taft from supporting black disfranchisement laws in his acceptance speech. Although Taft asked Washington to be his unofficial advisor, he stopped appointing blacks in the South and gradually removed those already there. However, Taft appointed a black as assistant attorney general – the highest rank yet attained by a black official. Taft also appointed blacks to diplomatic posts in African countries.

1912 saw the election of the first Southerner as President since the Civil War. Woodrow Wilson wanted nothing to do with Booker T. Washington. Wilson wanted to introduce Southern-style segregation to the civil service. His officials conducted investigations which concluded that white government workers were suffering. White women were 'forced unnecessarily to sit at desks with colored women' and,

ı   the same toilet is used by both whites and blacks, and some of the said blacks have been diseased, evidence thereof being very apparent; that one Negro women had been for years afflicted with a private disease, and for dread of using the toilet after her, some of the white girls are
5   compelled to suffer physically and mentally.[4]

Wilson agreed that toilet and eating facilities should be segregated and black men limited to jobs where they would not be in contact with white women. Washington and other black leaders protested but Wilson told them, 'Segregation is not humiliating but a benefit, and ought to be so regarded by you gentlemen.' He felt there was 'nothing to apologise for in the past of the South, including slavery, which had done more for the Negro in 250 years than African freedom had done since the building of the pyramids.' Wilson praised the Ku Klux Klan for helping save the South from black rule during Reconstruction. Wilson removed blacks from government positions. Many of them had been Washington's nominees. Southerners dominated Congress and had it not been for Washington's mobilisation of opposition, they would have passed a bill barring foreign-born blacks from immigration into the US. Thus Washington had mixed fortunes in his dealings with those in power in the nation's capital.

Like all famous men, Washington aroused hostility as well as admiration. Many whites resented and loathed him. A white chambermaid in an Indianapolis hotel was supposedly fired for refusing to make up Washington's bed, so a Texas newspaper fund-raised for this 'self-respecting girl'. As with Martin Luther King decades later, hostile whites grasped any opportunity to damage Washington's reputation, and were particularly keen to find 'evidence' of the excessive sexuality frequently attributed to blacks by whites. In 1911 Washington visited New York and claimed that he had got lost in an area frequented by prostitutes as he looked up an old friend. A white drunk attacked him there and accused him of theft. The drunk's 'wife' claimed Washington had said 'Hello, sweetheart' and tried to molest her. The newspapers believed her. Although Taft and Roosevelt spoke out for Washington, Washington's reputation suffered in the six months of legal wrangling. The court found him to be the guilty party.

Some believed that Washington did more harm than good for his fellow blacks. The Northern black press attacked Washington after the Atlanta Compromise speech. One black journalist called him 'the greatest white man's nigger in the world'. Some black reporters heckled Washington while he addressed black businessmen in Boston (1903). A riot ensued. Washington supported the arrest and prosecution of three reporters. That caused tension between Washington and the friend who was to become his most bitter rival, W.E.B. Du Bois.

c) Who Was Right – Booker T. Washington or Du Bois?

Du Bois and Washington initially worked together for the repeal of railroad [railway] segregation laws in Tennessee and for a New York conference to discuss black voting rights in the South (1904). They sought the same ultimate goal of equality for blacks, but advocated different tactics to achieve it. Why? They had very different backgrounds. Du Bois was born a free man in the North. He experienced relatively little racial prejudice until he attended Fisk, a Southern black university. He gained degrees from Harvard and Berlin, and in 1897 became professor of sociology at Atlanta University. Du Bois typified the elitist Northern black intellectuals, Washington the more pragmatic and lower class Southerners who had to coexist with whites. Washington believed whites would come around to accepting equal rights if blacks were peaceful, reasonable and made it clear they meant whites no harm. He wanted blacks to concentrate on improving their economic position, Du Bois believed that civil rights must be obtained first. He thought that without legal and political equality, economic prosperity could not be attained. Washington favoured 'separate but equal' as yet, while Du Bois at this stage sought rapid integration. Washington, frightened by the increasing number of lynchings, felt that Du Bois' more aggressive approach would only serve to alienate whites. The majority of blacks at the New York Conference supported Washington. In 1905 Du Bois called black leaders to a conference in Buffalo, New York. A racial incident in their Buffalo hotel caused them to move to the Canadian side of Niagara Falls where they established the Niagara Movement. The movement aimed to end inequality. Led by Du Bois, it pointedly excluded Washington. Washington was being superseded as a universally acknowledged black leader. The rivalry between the erstwhile friends became increasingly bitter. Washington employed detectives for protection and he and Du Bois had spies in each other's camp.

Some blacks felt that divisions among people like Du Bois and

Washington were damaging the black cause, but Washington stressed that Northern and Southern states required very different handling. His sharp distinction between racial problems in the North and the South meant that it was difficult to sustain his position as a national black leader. He was excluded by Du Bois from the National Negro Committee, which joined with the Niagara Movement (1909) and became the most famous black organisation of the twentieth century, the National Association for the Advancement of Colored People (NAACP). NAACP's declared aims were,

> to make 11,000,000 Americans physically free from peonage, mentally free from ignorance, politically free from disfranchisement, and socially free from insult.[5]

Relations between the new organisation and Booker T. Washington were not good. When President Wilson removed from office blacks who had been Washington's nominees, the NAACP did not object. NAACP concentrated on political and legal matters, while Washington helped to establish the National Urban League (1911) to help blacks adjust to urban life and to employment therein.

The increasing number of race riots across America worried Du Bois. In Springfield, Illinois, six blacks were killed by a white mob, and around 2000 more were driven out of Springfield (1908). Events such as the Springfield Riot moved Du Bois toward more confrontational strategies. As editor of the NAACP's newspaper *The Crisis*, Du Bois publicised riots and lynchings. He also tried to promote racial change through the law courts, all in a manner which Washington considered provocative. Du Bois considered Washington to be a self-seeking political in-fighter and master manipulator.

Washington's disagreements with Du Bois continued to the bitter end. In 1915, the movie *Birth of a Nation* was a great box-office success. It glorified the Ku Klux Klan. Du Bois and the NAACP called for a boycott of the movie, for which they blamed an upsurge in lynching. However, Washington said the call only gave the movie welcome publicity. He died soon after. By this time, most articulate blacks favoured Du Bois' social and political activism rather than Washington's accomodationism. Who do you think was right?

d) What was the Significance of Washington's Life and Career

Historians and contemporaries disagree over whether the situation of blacks deteriorated during the lifetime of Booker T. Washington, and whether he contributed to any deterioration by a misguided stance.

There was indeed 'disappointment' in the South. After emancipation, blacks had been given political equality, but disfranchisement and social segregation soon followed. Black leaders were divided over how to regain the rights fleetingly held during Reconstruction. Those divisions probably weakened their cause. Du Bois favoured vociferous campaigning for the full restoration of civil rights. Washington preferred to reassure and conciliate whites, while quietly campaigning against segregation and discrimination through the law courts, and stressing economic advancement. The white hostility he was facing can perhaps best be seen in his 'molestation' case.

In *The Souls of Black Folk* (1903), Du Bois acknowledged that Washington's rise to the position of 'the one recognised spokesman of his 10 million fellows' was 'the most striking thing in the history of the American Negro' since the end of Reconstruction. Du Bois said that while the elements of Washington's philosophy of 'industrial education, conciliation of the South, and submission and silence as to civil and political rights' were not original, Washington welded them

W.E.B. DU BOIS (1868–1963)   *-Profile-*

ISSUES

Why was Du Bois important? Why was he less influential than Washington?

Du Bois' frequent changes of mind (for example, on integration) and intellectual elitism help explain why he has been called 'a leader without followers'. He was prominent in establishing the most important twentieth century black organisation, the NAACP. He edited NAACP's magazine *Crisis* from 1909 to 1934, until his controversial advocacy of 'an economic Negro nation within a nation' forced him to resign. His articles were inspirational and provocative. He wrote effectively against lynching, and his assertions that blacks were a chosen people with special cultural and spiritual strengths contributed to the increased black pride manifested in the Harlem Renaissance (see page 38). Disillusioned by the slow pace of change in America, he emigrated to Africa (1961). There, he advocated Pan–Africanism (world black unity) and worked on the *Encyclopaedia Africana*. He joined the Communist Party in 1961. It was probably because he was unrealistic (he envisaged Africa populated by 'well–bred and courteous children, playing happily and never sniffing or whining'!) and uncompromising that Du Bois was less influential than Booker T. Washington was.

into an incredibly influential and coherent programme. Writing in the 1960s, African-American scholar Langston Hughes noted,

> historical and contemporary judgements affirm that Washington was in reality 'a great accomodator'. But to create Tuskegee in Alabama in that era he could hardly have been otherwise.[6]

There in perhaps lies a key to any assessment of Washington's contribution to black advancement: 'he could hardly have been otherwise.' His private papers reveal that while he gave whites the impression that he favoured segregation, he secretly financed and directed several court suits against segregation in Southern railroad facilities, wherein blacks were relegated to the worst carriages and rest rooms. He worked similarly against disfranchisement. Given the degree, extent and longevity of white hostility to blacks, 'accommodationism' probably stood more chance of consolidating black gains in America than confrontation – in his lifetime at least. He had impressed many whites with his achievements and moderation and won important recognition if inconsistent support from presidents and other politicians. He had increased the self-confidence of blacks by demonstrating that a black born in slavery could become a nationally and internationally respected figure, mixing with statesmen and monarchs. He had helped many individual blacks more directly through the Tuskegee Institute, and had encouraged white Southern acceptance of black access to education. His writings and actions artfully, carefully and patiently advertised black and white co-operation. His *Up From Slavery* deliberately avoided any residual bitterness about slavery and emphasised how many whites had helped and befriended him throughout his life. His life and career demonstrated that the situation of black Americans definitely improved after the Civil War.

2 Factors Leading Toward Change in the First Half of the Twentieth Century

> **KEY ISSUES** Which individuals, organisations and events contributed to black progress 1900–45? Who or what contributed most? How much progress was made?

In order to decide how much progress was made in the first half of the twentieth century, we need to remind ourselves of the situation for blacks around 1900. Blacks were frequently the victims of violence in the South. Public transport, churches, theatres, parks, beaches and schools were segregated. Blacks could not vote and their career opportunities remained limited. Historically and socially segregation was rooted in a desire to keep the best work and higher social status for whites and to ensure no dilution of the white race and its culture. Some whites were not totally committed to the status quo but fearful lest alterations caused trouble. Southern whites managed to cling on to their racist way of life through several methods. They dominated local politics. Long-standing Southern congressmen exploited seniority rules to maintain a tenacious grip on US Senate committees and used filibusters [prolonging congressional debates to stop bills being voted upon] and pragmatic alliances with Republicans to halt legislation that would help blacks. The power of the state governments, as opposed to the federal government, was vital for the continuation of white supremacy and discrimination. State governments controlled education, transportation and law enforcement. There was no federal [national] police force to protect blacks from discriminatory state laws in the South. Northern blacks suffered from social and economic inequality. Possession of the vote did not bring them great gains. The Republican party took black votes for granted.

Blacks throughout America usually had to seek their own solutions to their problems, assisted by external events and some whites. Black solutions included voting with their feet, developing a sense of community, and organised activism. They also benefited from events such as two world wars and the Depression.

a) The 'Great Migration'

Life was hard in the segregated South. There were limited opportunities for black economic advancement in what was already one of the poorest parts of America. One solution was the 'Great Migration'. Over 6 million blacks emigrated from the rural South to the great cities of the North, Mid-West and West between 1910 and 1970. In 1910, 89% of blacks lived in the South; by 1970 it was 53%. The industrial North offered greater economic opportunities, especially as European immigration decreased and World War One (1914–18) generated jobs. Southern blacks flocked to Northern cities like New York, Philadelphia, Chicago and the car-manufacturing centre of Detroit. Some sought labouring jobs in Southern cities.

Detroit Population Figures		
Year	Total population	Black population
1910	465,766	5741
1920	993,675	40,838
1930	1,568,662	120,066

(= 300% population increase, but 2400% black population increase)

The influx of blacks caused the deterioration of race relations in Northern cities where the Ku Klux Klan now appeared. In 1911 Baltimore passed its first residential segregation law. Other Northern cities followed suit. Competition for jobs and housing, along with resentment at increasing black political influence in local elections, led to serious racial violence in many cities. A primarily Southern race relations problem now become a national one. In Chicago, Irish and Polish workers, supported by the police and the military, committed appalling atrocities as they attacked blacks in the ghetto. However, urbanisation contributed greatly to the increase of black consciousness and a sense of community.

THE OTHER GREAT MIGRATION: HISPANICS

ISSUES

How, when and why did the US Hispanic population grow? In what ways was the Hispanics' experience similar to the blacks?

Hispanics settled in North America before other white Americans. When the US took over the American Southwest (what is now California, Arizona, New Mexico, and Texas), Mexicans were already in residence. During the twentieth century there was a massive influx of Hispanic immigrants seeking the greater economic opportunities offered in the United States. Some of the Hispanic immigrants came from Mexico, some from Puerto Rico (taken over by the US in 1898). Puerto Ricans began to immigrate to America, settling in New York in particular. In 1910, there were two thousand Puerto Ricans in the United States, rising to 53,000 in 1930. Cheap air travel after World War Two led to a total of one and a half million Puerto Ricans in the United States by 1970. A transport revolution was also important in the mass immigration of Mexicans to the United States in the twentieth century. In the early twentieth century, Mexicans arrived by and worked on the railroads. Mexicans were used to living without 'necessities' taken for granted by Americans, for example, running water and indoor toilets. Southwestern Americans therefore viewed the immigrants as undesirable and uncivilised. The Mexicans' customs, poverty, illiteracy, race, and lowly paid jobs set them apart from white Americans who, particularly in Texas, used segregation laws against them as against blacks.

b) World War One (1914–18)

World War One generated jobs and gave black soldiers who fought in France a glimpse of greater equality. Blacks found the French less racist than white Americans, who warned the French to keep their women away from black Americans who would probably rape them. German propaganda targeted blacks, urging them not to believe America's claim that it was fighting for democracy:

1   What is Democracy? Personal freedom, all citizens enjoying the same
    rights socially and before the law. Do you enjoy the same rights as the
    white people do in America, the land of Freedom and Democracy, or
    are you rather not treated over there as second-class citizens? Can you
5   go into a restaurant where white people dine? Can you get a seat in the
    theatre where white people sit? ... Is lynching and the most horrible
    crimes connected therewith lawful proceeding in the Democratic
    country?[7]

When mobilised blacks returned home white resentment at black competition for jobs and housing led to terrible race riots in 25 American cities (1919). The Chicago riots lasted a fortnight. 50,000 blacks had moved into Chicago between 1910 and 1920. White residents hated blacks moving into white neighbourhoods. When a 15 year-old black boy accidentally crossed the dividing line on a segregated beach that extended into Lake Michigan, whites stoned the boy. When blacks protested, the police arrested them. In the ensuing riots, 38 died and 500 were injured. The governor of Illinois commissioned a report. The report called for desegregation and blamed the riots on unfair treatment of blacks by white law enforcers, ghetto living conditions, and increasing black 'race consciousness'.

c) The Increasing Sense of Community

Segregation dramatically increased the black sense of community and unity in the face of white supremacy, as in 1938 when the 'Brown Bomber' Joe Louis defeated a white heavyweight boxer and became a world champion. Economic deprivation was another shared experience. The vast majority of blacks worked in low paid industrial, agricultural or domestic jobs. Black newspapers like the *Baltimore Afro-American* and *Pittsburgh Courier* increased the sense of community. There were also fraternal organisations, civic clubs and churches. Churches like the Abyssinian Baptist Church in Harlem, New York, provided the location, money and leadership for civic clubs wherein politics was discussed. Not all churches were hotbeds of civil rights activity, but most at least helped promote a spirit of self-help and self-confidence among blacks who easily identified with biblical stories of a chosen race who fled enslavement and went to the Promised Land. The black community's pride was increased by the

Harlem Renaissance (1919–30), wherein black intellectuals like the poet Langston Hughes and jazz musicians like 'Duke' Ellington flourished.
However, the black community was not always united. There were divisions of class, colour (light or dark skin), creed and career opportunities. A handful of black businessmen in cities such as Detroit and Chicago did well out of the segregation that gave them a captive market. Differences between the North and South hindered the development of black unity and caused black leaders like Booker T. Washington and Du Bois to disagree over how to improve the black lot. Du Bois worked to increase the sense of community through the NAACP, which attracted many middle-class blacks in the 1910s and 1920s, even in Southern cities. The black socialist A. Philip Randolph advocated another route. He established a black trade union for railroad porters (1925) and urged black workers to co-operate with white trade unionists. However, the individual most responsible for arousing black working class consciousness and awakening organisations such as NAACP to the need for wooing the working classes, was West Indian-born Marcus Garvey (1880–1940). Garvey's career illustrates black divisions, but also increasing black consciousness.

Between 1890 and 1920, New York City's black population increased from 70,000 to 200,000. Most were born in the South, but about 50,000 were born in the West Indies. Harlem was transformed from an all-white, fashionable upper class area into a densely populated black ghetto. African American and West Indian relations were tense. African Americans resented West Indians as clannish, over-ambitious, willing to work for lower wages, and unwilling to join black protest organisations. Marcus Garvey's career illustrates the hostility between African Americans and West Indians. The charismatic Jamaican-born Garvey advocated self-help and separation of races. He appealed to racial pride and (some said excessive) love of pageantry. His *Negro World* newspaper rejected advertisements for 'race-degrading' products that lightened skin and straightened hair. By 1925, urban blacks frustrated by the lack of progress after World War One swelled his Universal Negro Improvement Association (UNIA) membership to half a million, far more than the NAACP possessed. However, Garvey frightened and alienated many members of his race. Why? Other black leaders were jealous of this West Indian's appeal to the black American working classes, and, often light-skinned themselves, resented his claims that blacker was better. They particularly disliked his calls for the return of the 'best' (blackest) Americans to Africa (a place Garvey never visited). A light-skinned black Chicago doctor said UNIA really stood for 'Ugliest Negroes in America'. Du Bois called him 'a little, fat black man' and 'the most dangerous enemy of the Negro race' and Randolph's newspaper called him the 'Jamaican Jackass', 'monumental monkey' and 'unquestioned fool and ignoramus'. A black bishop publicly advocated that the

Communist Garvey should be deported. Garvey was found guilty of mail fraud, jailed (1923), then deported (1927). Garvey and his black critics actually had much in common: all advocated self-help and black racial pride and many were interested in internationalising the racial struggle. Despite these divisions among blacks, the sense of community was increasing under the pressure of urbanisation and frustration, and that sense of community would eventually facilitate more concerted black efforts to obtain equality.

d) What Had Been Achieved By 1930?

Individuals such as Garvey had helped raise black consciousness. The NAACP's anti-lynching campaign had publicised the horrors of lynchings and helped decrease their numbers. White supporters helped by claiming that lynchings damaged the South's image and progress. The NAACP had won a few court victories against the grandfather clause (1915), white domination of primaries and mob violence. However, the Southern caste system remained essentially intact. The

Two blacks are lynched before a satisfied white crowd, in the Northern state of Indiana, 1930.

National Urban League had done little to decrease black urban poverty in the North. Despite Randolph's encouragement, the majority of black workers were still not unionised.

Many blacks seemed apathetic. The Southern black middle class usually followed Booker T. Washington's 'accommodationist' ideas. A few joined the NAACP but the vast majority of blacks remained aloof from the reforming movements. Why? Blacks were preoccupied with earning a living and lacked any great tradition of political consciousness. Perhaps most important of all, Southern blacks knew that opposition to white supremacy could lead to death. Northern blacks were in a far better position to improve their status. They could vote, participate more easily in civic affairs, and had more economic opportunities. Despite police harassment and the Ku Klux Klan, Northern blacks lived in a far less violent society. Again, however, most Northern blacks concentrated upon improving their living standards. Some middle class professionals did join the NAACP or National Urban League, while working class blacks joined UNIA. However, black politicians who 'sold' black votes in return for personal gain often hampered idealistic black politicians.

By 1930 then, black activism had increased slightly and was better organised but activists were still a minority who as yet had done very little to end nation-wide segregation and discrimination. It took the Depression and the New Deal to bring about more dramatic change.

e) The Depression and the New Deal

In 1929 the New York stock market collapsed, triggering off years of economic depression in America. This Depression probably hit blacks harder than whites. Two million Southern black farmers left the land as crop prices plummeted. Many went to the cities where black unemployment was between 30% and 60% and always higher than that of whites. Desperate whites moved into the jobs formerly dominated by blacks, such as domestic service, street cleaning, garbage collection, and bellhops. Whites organised vigilante groups such as the Black Shirts of Atlanta to stop blacks getting jobs. As unskilled labour, blacks were usually last hired and first fired. There was no effective social security system, so disease and starvation frequently resulted.

In 1933, President Franklin Roosevelt began a hitherto unprecedented programme of government intervention to stimulate the economy and help the poor. The programme was called the New Deal. Before 1933 the federal government had appeared uninterested in blacks. Now New Deal programmes helped blacks by providing one million jobs, nearly 50,000 public housing units, and financial assistance and skilled occupations training for half a million black youths. As a result of federal assistance, many black sharecroppers (people who farmed the landowner's land and shared the profits from the land with him) became independent farmers. The New Deal provided jobs in the world of entertainment and culture, giving some black scholars the opportunity to increase black consciousness by getting black history and contemporary living conditions into the New Deal's State Guide books. Black songs and oral reminiscences of slavery and hardship were recorded for posterity. Government sponsorship of culture was inevitably controversial, and federal-funded biracial [black and white] dramatic productions were criticised by a congressional committee as encouraging black and white colleagues to go out on dates.

The New Deal could not guarantee miracles. Sometimes aid did not reach the persons for whom it was intended, particularly in the South where aid was distributed by whites. A leading New Dealer dismissed a black woman investigating black complaints against New Deal programmes because he felt it ridiculous to entrust a black with that particular job. However, New Dealers were often responsive to

HISPANIC AMERICANS – A COMPARISON

ISSUE

How did the Hispanics' situation compare to that of the blacks during the Depression?

The Depression severely damaged race relations between Americans and Hispanics. Most Mexican Americans were agricultural labourers, and US agriculture had been in depression since the 1920s. Many Mexicans were therefore on relief. High rates of crime and disease among the Mexicans further alienated white Americans. Mexicans were discriminated against and segregated in public places, such as restaurants and schools. Thus Hispanics, like blacks, suffered economic hardship and segregation in the Depression. However, unlike blacks, they could be deported. There were large-scale deportations of Mexican immigrants and even Mexican Americans who were American citizens. 16,000 were deported in 1931. The Mexican population of the United States, which was 600,000 in 1930, went down to 400,000 in 1940. As with black colonisation schemes in the nineteenth century, white Americans still favoured 'get rid of them' solutions to racial tensions. Expulsions continued after World War Two, with over one million Mexicans expelled in 1954. With blacks and Mexicans, white racism was usually due to rivalry over jobs, the belief that the non-whites were economically parasitical, and a dislike of the different style of living espoused by the ethnic minority.

criticism and even protest, as with the 1935 Harlem riot. One black died and 200 were injured in clashes with the police whom they believed to have beaten or possibly killed a young black shoplifter. While the tabloids tried to blame Communist agitators, an investigatory commission blamed Harlem's poverty and discrimination in relief given to blacks. Racist officials were transferred from Harlem and more local blacks were employed to administer relief.

The New Deal depended upon Southern white congressional votes, so Roosevelt left it to his wife to take a very public interest in black affairs. When a biracial group tried to hold a fully integrated meeting in Birmingham, Alabama (1938), even Birmingham's racist police chief Eugene 'Bull' Connor could not stop Eleanor Roosevelt sitting between the black and white delegates. The meeting did not condemn Jim Crow outright but declared support for equality before the law, voter registration for the poor, and funding for black post-graduates. Privately, Eleanor Roosevelt harangued New Deal officials into providing non-discriminatory aid for blacks. She introduced black representatives to her husband. There were nearly 50 blacks with relatively senior positions in the federal bureaucracy. They were nicknamed the 'Black Cabinet' because of their frequent meetings and concerted pressure on the administration.

What was the impact of the New Deal on blacks? New Deal agencies often discriminated against blacks, especially in the South, but blacks were getting more help and attention than ever before. Federal aid programmes helped many blacks, inspiring a dramatic change of allegiance amongst black voters. Previously the Democratic party had been associated in black minds with white supremacy, but now blacks voted for the party of Franklin Roosevelt. The increasing number of Northern black Democrats would soon make blacks a force to be reckoned with in the Party. This would be vital in the future acquisition of civil rights, although Roosevelt himself introduced no civil rights legislation. He denounced lynching as murder, but never fully supported anti-lynching bills of 1934, 1935 and 1938.

Roosevelt's New Deal had helped make civil rights a political issue. Not all Democrats were happy. Catering to the black vote, said one Southern Democrat, would lead to the 'depths of degradation' and 'mongrelisation of the American race'. White Southerners perceived an increase in black assertiveness and they blamed Roosevelt:

> You ask any nigger in the street who's the greatest man in the world. Nine out of ten will tell you Franklin Roosevelt. That's why I think he's so dangerous.[8]

Such white reactions suggest that the New Deal had contributed a great deal to the improvement and awareness of the black situation.

f) Trade Unionists and Left-wing Activists

Trade unionists, socialists and communists were important in raising black awareness of their potential political and economic power. Historically American trade unionism had been neither strong nor totally supportive of black workers. However, under pressure of the Depression trade unionism grew stronger. Black membership increased dramatically as trade unions for hitherto poorly organised unskilled workers developed. White working class racism still remained a great obstacle to interracial trade unionism, particularly in the South. However, the Depression helped to increase black and white working class solidarity.

Usually the more left-wing trade unions were the greatest supporters of equal rights, as with the Communist-dominated and 75% black FTA (Food, Tobacco, Agricultural and Allied Workers Union). The FTA promoted mass meetings that discussed voter registration and citizenship. Other left-led and predominantly black unions such as the United Packinghouse Workers of America did likewise.

Black intellectuals were impressed by the interracialism of the American Communist Party (CPUSA). CPUSA worked hard to win over blacks working in industry and agriculture in the early 1930s. The party helped Southern black agricultural workers to unionise, as in Lowndes County, Alabama. The unions were not always successful but Lowndes County became a civil rights centre in the 1960s, demonstrating how unionisation contributed to black assertiveness. The CPUSA provided legal help for the nine Scottsboro boys accused of raping two white women on an Alabama freight train in 1931, national press coverage of which made CPUSA look more effective than NAACP. CPUSA adapted their traditionally atheist message in the South, happily coexisting with black Christianity. In Winston-Salem, North Carolina, the Communist Party met in a black church, sang hymns and prayed. The Communist-dominated National Negro Congress aimed to promote equal civil and economic rights. A. Philip Randolph was its first elected president. It encouraged protest actions such as economic boycotts of stores that did not employ blacks, but the suspicious black churches and NAACP would not co-operate. Just how important were the black Communists? Historians disagree:

1 Party members such as [Hosea] Hudson tended to exaggerate the importance of the party in the 1930s and 1940s, claiming that it formed the basis for the civil rights movement of the following decades. Nell Painter discounts this claim, reminding us of the work of other groups
5 such as ... the Interracial Commission ... and the NAACP.[10]

g) NAACP Litigation and Legislation

In 1930 Walter White defeated Du Bois and became leader of the NAACP. White galvanised the NAACP into a campaign which helped

COMPARING BLACK AND RED

ISSUES

Was there a New Deal for Indians?
How did the red and black situations compare?

After the Indians had been put on reservations (see page 13), successive American governments either lacked interest in Indians, or were actively anti-Indian. As a Commissioner of Indian Affairs said in 1889,

> 1   The Indians must conform to 'the white man's ways,' peaceably if they will, forcibly if they must. They must ... conform their mode of living substantially to our civilisation. This civilisation may not be the best possible, but it is the best the Indians can get. They
> 5 can not escape it, and must either conform to it or be crushed by it.... The tribal relations should be broken up, socialism destroyed, and the family and the autonomy of the individual substituted.[9]

However, in the early twentieth century, federal government was more sympathetic. Why? The Indians' situation was clearly and frequently desperate. Their death rate exceeded their birth rate. Therefore, some white-dominated organisations publicised the plight of the Indians. However, only one of them opposed 'acculturation' (making Indians live like whites). Then, twenty-four unsolved murders of Oklahoma 'oil Indians' attracted massive publicity. Indian sympathisers believed whites who wanted the oil perpetrated the murders. The publicity forced the government to help the Oklahoma tribe. Other similar moves to take land from Indians in the 1920s were foiled due to publicity. A 1928 report commissioned by the federal government described Indian poverty, disease, and discontent, and shocked Americans. This prompted a Senate investigation.

Indians, like blacks, were greatly affected by two world wars and the Depression. In 1924 all Indians were guaranteed citizenship, primarily because so many had enlisted eagerly and distinguished themselves in World War One. Then Indians were particularly hard hit by the Depression. The Depression led white Americans to accept and expect more federal aid for the unfortunate. John Collier was one of the white intellectuals who were increasingly interested in the preservation of Indian culture. President F. D. Roosevelt appointed him Commissioner of Indian Affairs. Collier encouraged Congress to pass the Indian Reorganisation Act (1934), that started to restore tribal control over reservation land, and facilitated federal loans to struggling tribes. Collier continued the process whereby Indian school-children could attend local schools and learn about Indian culture. Schoolchildren were no longer forced to attend Christian services. Previously forbidden native religious observances were allowed on reservations. Collier influenced Congress to stop trying to halt Indian use of peyote, a hallucinatory substance obtained from a New Mexico cactus. Peyote was not addictive, did not induce violence, and Indians had traditionally used it to produce religious visions. Although some Christian missionaries, white exploiters, and anti-Communists opposed the restoration of Indian tribal culture, Collier had Roosevelt's total support.

Had Indians obtained a New Deal? Although the Indian Bureau employed more Indians, its white employees were frequently slow and unenthusiastic in implementing Collier's reforms. Nevertheless, thanks to federal intervention, Indians gained more land, greater farming expertise, better medical services, large federal money grants, and renewed pride in their traditions and culture. However, years of cultural persecution and deprivation made it difficult for the Indians to attain the full independence from Bureau control that Collier had envisaged. Much allotted land, for example, had been leased to whites. However, progress was made, thanks to a more enlightened government. The New Deal ethos continued for a time under Roosevelt's successor, President Truman. In 1946, Congress created the Indian Claims Commission, which adjudicated all claims arising out of fraud, treaty violations, or other wrongs done to Indians by the government. The Hoover Commission Task Force's admission (1948) that destroying Indian tribal government, organisation, property and culture 'now appears to have been a mistake' seemed to confirm that Indians, like blacks, had benefited from the New Deal. However, like blacks, Indians depended heavily upon federal aid for further improvements.

to stop an opponent of black voting become a Supreme Court judge (1930). He tried to organise a civil rights coalition between trade unions, churches and liberals. Sustained pressure from White's NAACP and liberal white allies led the House of Representatives to pass anti-lynching bills in 1937 and 1940, but Southern influence halted the bills in the Senate. The NAACP worked to mobilise Southern blacks. Revitalised Southern urban branches supported voter registration and abolition of the poll tax. In 1941 the NAACP, trade unions and the National Negro Congress sponsored a National Committee to Abolish The Poll Tax. NAACP was clearly changing. It was increasingly activist and co-operating with other groups in an emergent civil rights coalition. It was also altering its legal tactics.

In the 1920s the NAACP had worked against a wide range of civil rights abuses. From 1931 it concentrated on obtaining a Supreme Court ruling that unequal expenditure on black and white education was against the Fourteenth Amendment. After two white lawyers refused the job, black law professor Charles Houston of Howard University was appointed to direct the NAACP's legal campaign in 1934. Houston insisted that the NAACP should employ black lawyers. At Howard he had trained a black lawyer elite for this task. In 1936 the NAACP hired his star pupil, Thurgood Marshall ('lean, hard, and Hollywood handsome' according to Roy Wilkins). Houston and Marshall led the fight against segregated education in the 1930s and 1940s, working to involve black communities in litigation at local level. Marshall argued for equal salaries for black teachers in Maryland and Virginia (1935–40). Most black teachers feared dismissal but a few came forward and gained legal victories. Houston targeted a Supreme Court liberalised by New Deal appointments. He focused first on graduate schools, believing they were an easier target than the larger and more high profile public schools. The Supreme Court decreed that blacks had the right to the same quality of graduate education as whites. The NAACP was slowly but successfully encouraging change in America.

h) The Impact of World War Two (1939–45)

The war brought great changes to America, and this affected blacks. As defence industries became vitally important and Southern farming became more large scale and mechanised, blacks gravitated to the cities. Around 4 million blacks left Southern farms. Nearly half of them migrated North and West. Chicago's black population rose from around a quarter of a million in 1940 to nearly half a million in 1950.

The war increased black consciousness. Urban housing shortages were acute as people crowded into the cities. City authorities were unsympathetic to the plight of transplanted Southern blacks, and if help was given, it was usually for whites. Washington DC's black community suffered as the federal bureaucracy physically expanded. Several hundred black homes were demolished to make way for the War Department's Pentagon building and for the extension of Arlington National Cemetery. In crowded wartime cities, blacks and whites found themselves in closer proximity than usual. This caused tension, especially in the South. There were numerous acts of defiance on overcrowded buses, as when a New Orleans driver ordered a black soldier to sit at the back of the bus, which lead to the arrest of all 24 black passengers (1943). There was tension in the workplace. At the Alabama Dry Dock Company in Mobile in 1943, white workers (male and female) lashed out at black workers with any 'weapons' they could lay their hands on, including bricks and tools. 50 were injured. Why? There was jealousy over the best jobs and white males disliked black men working alongside white women. Southern military bases containing Northern black soldiers were trouble spots. In Alexandria, Louisiana, a drunken black soldier's arrest led to a two-hour riot in which black troops, white Military Police, state troopers, local police and civilians participated. 13 blacks were shot. There was massive enlistment in the NAACP. NAACP numbers increased from 50,000 to 450,000 (1940–5). Most of the new members were Southern professionals (one third of NAACP members were Southern) but co-operation with trade unions also brought in urban workers. Close co-operation between the NAACP and trade unionists proved productive, as in New Orleans where it radicalised the NAACP leadership into effective work on school equalisation and voter registration (1941).

Northern blacks campaigned for greater equality in the war. They cited American anti-fascist propaganda such as the Atlantic Charter, which called for freedom and equality. They pointed out that America itself had not yet attained true democracy when Southern blacks could not vote. Wartime demand for black labour gave black workers greater bargaining power. Randolph threatened to bring Washington DC to a standstill unless there was equality within the armed forces and the workplace. Impatient at the lack of progress on an anti-lynching law, Walter White was supportive. On the advice of his generals, Roosevelt refused to integrate the armed forces, but he set up a federal agency called the Committee on Fair Employment Practices (FEPC) to promote equality in defence industries. It seemed that direct action paid off. Randolph organised a March on Washington, but NAACP were jealous and disliked his exclusion of whites, so Randolph failed to gain great support.

Some blacks were inspired by Gandhi's confrontational but non-violent tactics against the British in India. The Howard-educated Christian Socialist James Farmer thought such tactics would be particularly effective in wartime, and advocated a campaign of 'relentless non-co-operation, economic boycott, civil disobedience'. In 1942 Farmer established the Congress of Racial Equality (CORE) which organised sit-ins at segregated Chicago restaurants and demanded desegregation on interstate transport. In 1941, Reverend Adam Clayton Powell, Jr, of the Abyssinian Baptist Church of Harlem led a successful bus boycott to force the company to employ more blacks.

A black activist said most blacks considered activism as eccentric. Most blacks remained quiescent in World War Two, not wanting to appear unpatriotic and fearing disorder, especially after violent race riots in Detroit and Harlem in summer 1943. Those riots convinced many blacks that Randolph and the radicals were irresponsible. Wartime prosperity also militated against activism.

What then had been achieved in World War Two? Greater black urbanisation (especially in the North) increased awareness and activism. Inspired by America's fight against fascism abroad, direct action was increasing and was instrumental in the establishment of FEPC. FEPC accomplished just enough to show the importance of federal aid but too little to be considered a great success. Two thirds of the 8000 job discrimination cases referred to FEPC were dismissed and only one fifth of Southern cases were black victories. Southern

ASIAN AMERICANS – A COMPARATIVE STUDY

ISSUE

What does the treatment of Asian Americans, especially in World War Two, reveal about racism and race relations in America?

The United States stopped Chinese immigration in 1882, Japanese immigration in 1907, and immigration by all other Asian Pacific peoples in 1917. What caused this racial hostility? White Americans were suspicious of the different appearance and culture of Asians. For example, Americans disliked it when Japanese or Chinese males in the United States chose a bride from the home country by looking at photographs. Furthermore, the prevalence of single Chinese males in turn-of-the-century America led to the rise of notorious 'Chinatowns', for example in San Francisco. Lurid stories about gang warfare, opium dens and vice districts in Chinatowns turned many Americans against the Chinese. Asian Americans, like Hispanics, became most unpopular during periods of economic Depression. In the 1930s, for example, Filipinos were deported. The Filipinos, although not technically alien (the Philippines were part of the American Empire) were rivals for jobs and therefore had to go.

One of the most famous examples of racial hostility in United States was the hostility toward West Coast Japanese Americans after the Japanese bombing of Pearl Harbor brought the United States into World War Two (1941). 110,000 Japanese Americans were interned in concentration camps spread across the United States. Two thirds of them were US citizens, yet they were deprived of property and freedom, and treated as prisoners of war. Although the United States was simultaneously at war with Germany, no such actions were taken against German Americans. However, despite this treatment, Japanese Americans soon recovered to be one of the most prosperous US ethnic groups, earning on average today far more than Americans of British ancestry do. This has led the historian Thomas Sowell[12] to conclude that racism and persecution alone do not explain poverty.

congressmen successfully decreased FEPC funding after it was given greater power in 1943. The battle against employment discrimination had to be taken up by Randolph, then the NAACP and trade unionists, who had little success until the 1960s. On the other hand, the potential importance of federal aid was undeniable. The increasingly sympathetic US Justice Department had set up a Civil Rights Section, which tried to decrease lynching and police brutality in the South. Southern black political rights increased thanks to a 1944 Supreme Court decision (SMITH v. ALLWRIGHT). The decision resulted from the NAACP's Texas campaign against white primaries. The Supreme Court declared the exclusion of blacks from the primaries unconstitutional under the Fifteenth Amendment. The scholar D.C. Hine described the SMITH decision as 'the watershed in the struggle for black rights'.[11] Segregationists resorted to illegality to stop blacks voting, but between 1940 and 1947 the number of black registered voters increased in the South from 3% to 12%. Most of these gains seemed irrelevant as yet to the majority of Southern blacks. They watched the increased activism with interest, but rejected militancy, lest it alienate Southern white liberals. However, things would never be the same again. In a war against a racist German regime, black Americans fought in a segregated American army, frequently led by white officers. As demobilised white servicemen returned, disproportionate numbers of blacks were fired from their wartime jobs. The segregated armed forces damaged the morale of some blacks but increased the incentive for change for others. It was hundreds of ex-servicemen who bravely tried to thwart the election of a racist Mississippi senator in 1946.

3 Conclusions

> **KEY ISSUES** How much had been achieved by 1945?
> Who or what was responsible for the achievement?

In 1900 blacks constituted an economic and social under-class throughout America, but particularly in the South where they lacked any political power. Blacks lacked nationally known and recognised organisations and leaders, apart from Booker T. Washington. By 1945 there had been a clear and dramatic increase in black consciousness and activism. Although segregation and political inequality remained in the South, Southern white supremacy was being slowly and painfully eroded by a series of legal decisions. Now black organisations used a combination of co-operation, coercion and confrontation when dealing with whites. The number of significant black leaders was increasing, although they had frequent disagreements over the means to the commonly desired end of greater equality for blacks.

How had this happened? Partly through the work of black and white individuals, such as Booker T. Washington, A. Philip Randolph, W.E.B. Du Bois, Walter White, and Eleanor Roosevelt. Washington had shown what a black person could achieve. When his achievements, writings and speeches made him the recognised spokesman for his race, he gained access to successive presidents. Sometimes presidents worked with him, sometimes they worked against him, but they always took notice of him. As time passed, and there was no marked improvement in the position of blacks, leading spokesmen became more militant. However, the early twentieth century was not ready for Du Bois' calls for greater civil rights activism. Other black leaders preferred to work through organisations, for example Randolph and trade unions, and Walter White and the NAACP. It was perhaps the organisations, rather than the individuals, which had the greatest potential to mobilise black people. The NAACP worked with quiet tenacity in the first half of the twentieth century, and would provide the elements of continuity and respectability that come with longevity. The NAACP increased the awareness and activism of many blacks. American ideals were important. Given all the talk of freedom, democracy and equality in the history of WHITE America, it was inevitable that the position of blacks should increasingly be perceived as anomalous. External events were important. Under the impact of two world wars, blacks moved into the cities where there was greater opportunity for economic gain and for education in political and social inequalities and ways to combat them. The wars and the

Segregated water fountain, North Carolina.

Depression finally galvanised the federal government into actions that benefited blacks. It was perhaps the involvement of the federal government – at last – which was the single most important factor in improving the black situation. While individual states continued to decide the fate of Southern blacks in particular, there was little hope for improvement. However, once the federal government took upon itself clear and consistent responsibility for that improvement, the days of state power would be limited. In some ways the federal intervention came about by accident. Federal aid to the poor in the 1930s inevitably meant federal aid to a great many blacks, most of whom were amongst the poorest of Americans. The foundations of the great civil rights movement of the mid-twentieth century had been laid.

References

1 For details see *Booker T. Washington: Up From Slavery*, OUP, 1995, p. vii.
2 Quoted in J. Neyland, *Booker T. Washington*, Holloway House Publishing Co., 1992, pp. 117–8.
3 Quoted in John White, *Black Leadership in America*, Longman, 1994, p. 29.
4 Quoted in Peter Carroll and David Noble, *The Free and the Unfree*, Penguin Putnam Inc., 1988, p. 255.
5 *Black Leadership*, p. 50.
6 Quoted on p. xxi, *Up From Slavery*.
7 Quoted in John Hope Franklin and Alfred Moss, *From Slavery To Freedom*, McGraw-Hill, 1998, p. 333.
8 Quoted in A.J. Badger, *The New Deal*, Macmillan, 1989, p. 271.
9 Quoted in Alvin Josephy, *500 Nations*, New York, 1994, p. 431.
10 Quoted in *From Slavery to Freedom*, by John Hope Franklin and Alfred Moss, both of whom are black historians, pp. 387–8.
11 Quoted in Robert Cook, *Sweet Land of Liberty?*, Longman, 1998, p. 81.
12 Thomas Sowell, *Ethnic America*, Basic Books, 1981, chapter 7 *et passim*.

Summary Diagram

Who/What Contributed to the Black Awakening, 1900–45

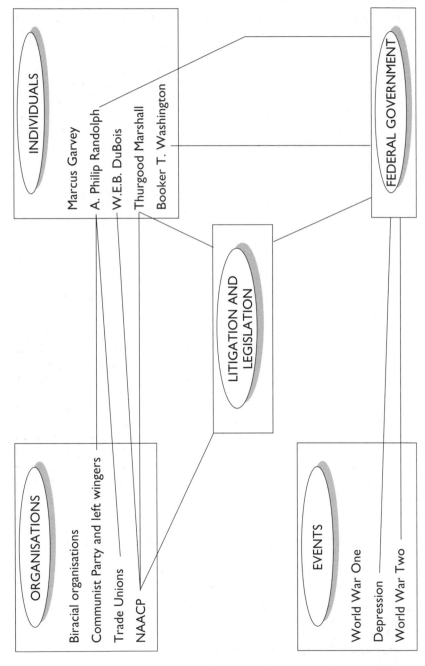

Working on Chapter 3

In this chapter you have studied 'progress', but whenever you study 'progress', you have to ask whether the situation improved consistently, and whether it improved for everyone.

You also need to ask who contributed most to the progress and to the lack of it, so you could make your notes in grid form, with columns headed by some landmark success or failure, then INDIVIDUALS, EVENTS, ORGANISATIONS, FEDERAL GOVERNMENT as your side headings. Then a pattern might emerge suggesting who or what is most responsible for progress (or the lack of it).

Answering structured and essay questions on Chapter 3

Think about these structured questions:

a) How much did Booker T. Washington achieve for blacks? (*10 marks*)
b) Who or what stopped him achieving more? (*8 marks*)
c) Which individual, in the quarter of a century after the death of Booker T. Washington, was most responsible for improving the position of blacks in American society? (*7 marks*)

Examiners design questions so that they differentiate between candidates. The attention paid by candidates to 'how much' in (a) will be vital in deciding the candidate's final grade. If someone simply reels off the list of positive achievements, they will probably get grade D. The candidate who also gives negative points about Washington, and the things he failed to do, should get a higher grade. Similarly, 'which individual' is a nice trap designed for those who only know and want to talk about one individual. It is better to make frequent contrasts and comparisons with other likely contenders. You might choose President Roosevelt as the individual who did most, but you should also explained why you reject Du Bois, A. Philip Randolph, and Marcus Garvey.

Answering source-based questions on Chapter 3

Look at the source extracts on pages 28, 30, 32, 34, 37 and 43, then think about the following questions:

a) What did the NAACP (page 32) mean by
   (i) 'physically free from peonage'?
   (ii) 'mentally free from ignorance'?
   (iii) 'politically free from disfranchisement'?
   (iv) 'socially free from insults'? (*4 marks*)

b) Does the German propaganda (page 37) use language, tone, and content effectively? (*4 marks*)
c) Given the traditional American hatred of Communism, who would you consider to be the more reliable source for a historian assessing the importance of black Communism to the civil rights movement (page 43), Hosea Hudson or Franklin and Moss (all of whom are black)? (*6 marks*)
d) Using the sources and your own knowledge, would you agree that Booker T. Washington 'could hardly have been otherwise' throughout his career? (*6 marks*)

Whenever you are asked about 'language and tone', it is always helpful to use an adjective before those key words throughout your answer. For example, you might consider the Germans were using a 'sarcastic tone' when they talk of freedom in a country wherein races were unequal.

'Reliability' questions usually (but not always) give you pointers as to 'reliability for what?' So, you always need to think about the exact issue a historian is considering. A source can be reliable in some ways but not in others. For example, a source that totally dismisses the importance of Communism in the black civil rights struggle is reliable evidence for the historian seeking to prove America's fanatical anti-communism, but it is not reliable evidence for the help that the Communist Party gave to blacks.

The Start of the Civil Rights Movement 1945–1960

4

POINTS TO CONSIDER

From 1945 to 1960, consciousness of racial inequalities increased rapidly. Some improvements were made. This chapter seeks to explain why. You should consider which individuals, which organisations, and which laws are the most important in helping and hindering change.

KEY DATES

1947 Truman administration report, '*To Secure These Rights*'.
1948 Truman tried to end discrimination in federal employment.
1950 Supreme Court virtually overturned PLESSY v. FERGUSON.
1954 Supreme Court declared against segregated schools (BROWN). White Citizens Councils formed throughout South.
1955 May – Supreme Court urged desegregation of education (BROWN II).
1956 Montgomery Bus Boycott.
1957 Civil Rights Act. Desegregation controversy Little Rock, Arkansas.
1958 Supreme Court declared school segregation unconstitutional (COOPER v. AARON).

When President Franklin D. Roosevelt died in office in 1945, Vice-President Harry Truman became president. Truman was then elected president in his own right in 1948. Truman's life and career illustrate race relations in the first half of the twentieth century. Truman is particularly interesting because he appeared to develop from racist into statesman on the civil rights issue.

1 President Truman's Early Life and Career

KEY ISSUE In what ways do Truman's early life and career illustrate American race relations?

Born and raised in late nineteenth century Missouri, it would have been unusual if Harry Truman had not been racist. The centre of his hometown of Independence, Missouri (population 6000) had the dirt streets and violence of the Western frontier town. Away from the centre were elm tree lined streets with nice houses where families of North European ancestry such as the Trumans lived. Nostalgia for the

Confederacy was great in Independence. Most of the black residents over 40 had been born in slavery. Blacks lived in the shacks of ' Nigger Neck' in northeast Independence. They were responsible for frequent nighttime hold-ups and burglaries. They were unwelcome in most stores, not allowed in the town library, and had a separate school. Words such as 'nigger' and 'coon' were commonly used, and Harry Truman was no exception to the norm. The local press reported any lynching in the South in lurid detail, always indicating that the victims deserved their fate. In 1901, the schoolboy Harry Truman could have read the following local editorial:

1 The community at large need not be especially surprised if there is a Negro lynching in Independence. The conditions are favourable at this time. There are a lot of worthless young Negro men in town who do nothing. They do not pretend to work and stand around on the streets
5 and swear and make remarks about ladies and others who may pass by. They crowd into the electric cars and become offensive.[1]

However, local editors admitted that there were many blacks who were 'good citizens' and would reject the 'worthless' as much as any white.

Truman's ancestors had owned slaves. His uncle was a thug who shot some blacks 'to see them jump'. The young Harry Truman first met blacks as family servants. Harry told his sweetheart Bess that one man was as good as another, 'so long as he is honest and decent and not a nigger or a Chinaman'. He told her of his Confederate uncle who hated

Chinks [Chinese] and Japs. So do I. It is race prejudice I guess. But I am strongly of the opinion that Negroes ought to be in Africa, yellow men in Asia, and white men in Europe and America.[2]

When Truman went off to fight to 'make the world safe for democracy' in World War One, he sailed from New York which he felt had too many Jews (he called it 'Kike [Jew] town') and 'Wops' (Italians). In all this, he was typical of his era. Early in his political career he did what many aspiring politicians did and paid $10 membership dues to the Ku Klux Klan, but apparently got his money back when he insisted on the right to appoint Catholics as well as Protestants to office.

Once in national politics, Truman seemed to change. As president he helped blacks more than any of his recent predecessors had done.

2 How Much Did Truman Help Blacks?

KEY ISSUES How much did Truman help promote racial equality through legislation or executive action?

In the Senate in the late 1930s, Truman consistently supported legislation to abolish the poll tax and stop lynching. In his 1940 campaign for reelection to the Senate he made what was a very radical speech for Missouri in that era. He told his predominantly white audience:

> I I believe in the brotherhood ... of all men before the law.... If any [one]
> class or race can be permanently set apart from, or pushed down below
> the rest in politics and civil rights, so may any other class or race ... and
> we may say farewell to the principles on which we count our safety....
> 5 The majority of our Negro people find but cold comfort in shanties and
> tenements. Surely, as free men, they are entitled to something better
> than this.[3]

As president, Truman did nothing significant to help blacks at first. In 1945 for example, the FEPC (see pages 47–49) tried to end discriminatory hiring policies by a Washington DC transportation company. Although the FEPC had succeeded in 16 other Northern and Western cities, Truman gave them no real help in Washington. He did try to get Congress to continue funding the FEPC but they refused. Then, in 1946, President Truman established a liberal civil rights committee to investigate increasing violence against blacks. He deliberately chose liberals to be on the committee, ensuring that their report would draw national attention to unacceptable situations.

In October 1947 the committee gave Truman their report, entitled '*To Secure These Rights*'. It said the United States could not claim to be the democratic leader of the free world while some of its people were not treated as equals. The report advocated eliminating segregation from American life by using federal power. It called for: anti-lynching legislation; abolition of the poll tax; voting rights statutes; a permanent FEPC; an end to discrimination in interstate travel; an end to discrimination in the armed forces; a civil rights division in the Justice Department; administration support for civil rights suits in the federal court; the establishment of the United States Commission on Civil Rights.

These recommendations were revolutionary in a country where relations between blacks and whites were so tense that segregation was still legally enforced in all the former states of the Confederacy, and, in slightly less extreme form, in Maryland, West Virginia, Kentucky and Truman's home state of Missouri. In the North and West, while not legally enshrined, segregation was a social fact. New York's Brooklyn Dodgers had just introduced the first black baseball player to the major league. Jackie Robinson's presence caused antagonism amongst fans and players throughout the North. Southerners and even some Northerners referred to grown black males as 'boy'. In the movies, black characters were often wide-eyed, slow-witted buffoons. Nevertheless Truman went ahead, implementing the changes that were within his power and calling for the changes the report recommended in his State of the Union addresses in 1947 and 1948.

In his 1948 State of the Union address, Truman said 'our first goal' must be 'to secure fully the essential human rights of our citizens'. He pointed out the disparity between the words of America's Founding Fathers ('all men are created equal') and the actions of their descendants. He said it was important to set a good example to a Cold War world faced with the choice between American-style freedom and Soviet-style enslavement. He called for civil rights legislation as recommended in *To Secure These Rights*.

In the presidential election year of 1948, despite dissent within his own party and Republican antagonism, Truman suddenly issued executive orders to end discrimination in the armed forces and guarantee fair employment in the civil service. However, the army top brass resisted for as long as they dared (over two years) and initially there were few black officers. Furthermore, the National Guard and the reserves remained segregated. Similarly, although his Fair Employment Board (established in 1948) was designed to give minorities equal treatment in federal hiring, it was handicapped by shortage of funds, and conservative employees. However, its mere existence affirmed federal commitment to the principle of equality and set an example to other employers.

Truman appointed a black judge to the federal courts and a black Governor of the Virgin Isles. He tried to use federal purchasing power to prompt other employers to work toward equality. By Executive Order 10308 (December 1951) he established a Committee on Government Contract Compliance (CGCC). Federal defence contracts were not supposed to be given to companies that discriminated against minorities. However, as the CGCC could only recommend not enforce, it was even less effective than FEPC. This angered black activists, but Truman could not afford to antagonise Congress during the Korean War. The *Pittsburgh Courier* recognised CGCC was the best Truman could do 'under the circumstances'. It was the forerunner of more effective committees under subsequent presidents.

Truman wanted to give greater federal aid to impoverished blacks. He tried to open more public housing to blacks after 1948. However, the administration's urban renewal programme often left blacks homeless. There were usually fewer homes available in the new and more spacious public housing units than in the slums they replaced.

Perhaps the most important thing Truman had done (more than any president since Lincoln) was to awaken America's conscience to civil rights issues, through his speeches and symbolic actions. Small steps, such as integrated inauguration celebrations in January 1949 and the desegregation of Washington DC Airport, served collectively to make an important point.

Things could not and would not be changed overnight. Congress resisted Truman's civil rights legislative programme. Polls in 1949–50 showed that while many voters favoured abolition of the poll tax, only 33% favoured the fair employment bill. However, Truman's words and deeds had given clear signals that things must be changed.

3 What Motivated Truman?

KEY ISSUE Did Truman simply want the black vote?

We have seen that Harry Truman appeared to modify his views on non-whites during the course of his life and career. This raises questions as to his motivation. Were his motives purely political? Or did events, age and responsibility combine to make him more sympathetic to ethnic minorities? It is possible that while Truman remained a racist at heart, he knew that racism was wrong and should be combated by those in power. Having studied Truman's political career, you can make up your mind as to whether it illustrates how important the black vote had become, or illustrates changing American attitudes.

a) Race and Votes

As a Missouri senator, Truman still used the word 'nigger' privately and made racist jokes, even as he favoured legislation to help blacks. So did Truman simply change his stance because blacks were increasingly important Democratic voters? There were fewer black voters than white voters in Missouri, so espousal of the black cause would not have helped him gain more votes in his home state. On the other hand, any astute politician like Truman had to be aware that race relations were becoming increasingly important in a politician's career. In 1944 President Roosevelt considered Truman as a vice presidential running mate. Truman's main rival was quite openly racist and complained bitterly that

> the Negro has come into control of the Democratic party ... Mr President, all I have heard around this White House for the last week is nigger. I wonder if anybody thinks about the white people.[4]

Roosevelt chose Truman as his vice-president partly because he had 'never made' any such 'racial remarks' – at least, not publicly.

When Roosevelt died, Vice-President Truman became president. Initially he was not helpful to blacks, as with FEPC (see pages 57–58). Does his personal ambivalence on race relations explain his half-hearted commitment to FEPC? It is more likely that he felt that as the voters had not elected him president he needed to be cautious over controversial issues. Just how sensitive the race issue was can be seen in the Trumans' clash with the Daughters of the American Revolution (a society whose members could claim American ancestry back to the revolutionary war era). In 1945 the DAR refused to allow black Representative Adam Clayton Powell's black wife (a musician) to perform in their hall. Powell therefore asked Mrs Bess Truman to boycott a DAR tea. Bess said that although she deplored the treatment of Mrs Powell she would attend the tea. Powell described the First Lady as 'the last lady of the land', which infuriated ultra-loyal Harry. Truman privately christened Powell ' a smart aleck and a rabble rouser' and refused to receive him at the White House. The whole affair showed how racial discrimination had achieved a higher profile, what a struggle it was to reject racist traditions, and how difficult it was for any politician let alone the president (and his wife) to keep all races happy. However, in September 1946 Truman appointed a liberal civil rights committee to investigate increasing violence against blacks (see page 57). Although Walter White and Truman's advisers felt the committee 'was nothing short of political suicide' Truman told his aide to 'push it with everything you have'. In his 1947 and 1948 State of the Union addresses, Truman urged the civil rights legislation recommended by the committee. This risked splitting his party and damaging his chances of getting elected in 1948. Why did he do it?

Truman thought that progress on civil rights would be a Cold War propaganda victory. Perhaps more importantly, some Democrats such as New York's boss Ed Flynn wanted the black vote. There was political advantage to Truman's liberalism on civil rights. His advisers told him that many believed 'the Northern Negro vote today holds the balance of power in presidential elections' because the blacks voted as a block and were geographically concentrated in pivotal large and closely-contested electoral states like New York, Illinois and Michigan.

However, there were political disadvantages in seeking civil rights legislation. Although Truman reminded them that his Missouri background led him to sympathise with them, Southern Democrats were furious. One refused to attend a dinner with Truman in case he was seated alongside a 'Nigra'. Polls showed only 6% of voters supported a civil rights programme. Not surprisingly, Truman made only one civil rights speech during the presidential campaign and that was in Harlem! Controversy erupted during the Democratic Convention. Minneapolis Mayor Hubert Humphrey rejected the party's civil rights plank, designed in 1944 to appease Southern whites. Humphrey advocated adopting Truman's new programme, saying,

> There are those who say to you – we are rushing this issue of civil rights. I say we are 172 years too late.... The time has arrived for the Democratic Party to get out of the shadow of states rights and walk forthrightly into the bright sunshine of human rights.[5]

Northerners and Westerners cheered in the aisles, but Southerners stayed glumly seated. While Humphrey probably contributed greatly to Truman's election by ensuring a large black vote, Truman criticised Humphrey's group as 'crackpots' who split the party. Southern Democrats nominated Strom Thurmond as their candidate for president. Thurmond's 'Dixiecrat' platform advocated segregation and the 'racial integrity of each race'. Strom Thurmond thought it was 'un-

American' to force 'us' to 'admit the Negro into our homes, our eating places, our swimming pools and our theatres'. One Alabama Dixiecrat denounced Truman's civil rights programme as an attempt 'to reduce us to the status of a mongrel, inferior race'. When Truman then moved to end discrimination in the armed forces and civil service, he probably calculated that as he had already lost the extremist white vote, he might as well ensure the liberal and black vote. He was also under pressure from A. Philip Randolph's call for a black draft-resistance movement (a frightening prospect as the Cold War got underway). Also, these reforms could be done on the president's authority, which helped show up the uncooperative Republican Congress.

Truman's stance required considerable courage. In the face of Dixiecrat threats that 'they would shoot Truman, that no-good son-of-a-bitch and his civil rights', Truman campaigned in Texas where racial hatred was often intense. He was booed in Waco when he shook hands with a black woman, although segregation was abolished for the day in Dallas Rebel Stadium where blacks and whites cheered him. It was a political gamble to show support for blacks in the South especially as Truman's ideas were deliberately misrepresented. His advocacy of equality of opportunity was interpreted as advocacy of racial miscegenation and inter-marriage. Integrated political meetings in Southern states sometimes led to serious violence. In Memphis the local political 'Boss' tried to stop the black singer and actor Paul Robeson addressing an integrated Progressive rally. The Ku Klux Klan surrounded the several thousand strong crowd but dared not attack because 100 armed blacks stood alongside them. Given this background, there must surely have been an important element of idealism in Truman's stance.

In the election, Truman carried an unprecedented two thirds of the black vote. The black vote played a big part in getting him elected, especially in crucial states like California and Illinois. So was that why Truman had apparently changed his position on blacks? Surely not. After all, the South was traditionally and solidly Democrat, and Truman's civil rights advocacy cost him the 'Dixiecrat vote' which was probably as numerically significant as the black vote. Furthermore, once elected, he continued to prod America toward a fairer society. As he told his racist sister, he really believed that such changes were essential for America's national well-being, in respect of law and order, economic advancement and its proclaimed leadership of the free world against Communism. Truman's motivation was not purely political.

b) Truman's Other Motives

Truman was racist but he tried to be fair. He did not seek social equality for blacks, but he wanted legal equality, which was the black man's basic right, 'because he is a human being and a natural born

American.' Like many contemporaries, he was horrified by attacks on black servicemen returning from World War Two. The worst attacks were in the Deep South. Truman described how his stomach

> turned over when I learned that Negro soldiers, just back from over-seas, were being dumped out of army trucks in Missouri and beaten. Whatever my inclinations as a native of Missouri might have been, as President I know this is bad. I shall fight to end evils like this.... I am
> 5 not asking for social equality, because no such things exist, but I am asking for equality of opportunity for all human beings.... When a mayor and a City Marshal can take a Negro Sergeant off a bus in South Carolina, beat him up and put out one of his eyes, and nothing is done about it by the State Authorities, something is radically wrong with the system.[6]

Truman recognised that, regardless of race, the general principle of respect for the law was at stake. Privately he still spoke of 'niggers' and his sister claimed that 'Harry is no more for nigger equality than any of us'. Publicly he told Southern friends they were 'living 80 years behind the time' and for the good of America they had better change. The distance travelled by the racist from Missouri could be seen in June 1947 when he told his sister:

> I have got to make a speech to the Society for the Advancement of Colored People tomorrow, and I wish I didn't have to make it. Mrs Roosevelt [who is also speaking] has spent her public life stirring up trouble between white and black – and I am in the middle. Mamma won't
> 5 like what I say because I wind up by quoting old Abe [Abraham Lincoln]. But I believe what I say and I am hopeful we may implement it.[7]

On the steps of Washington DC's Lincoln Memorial and before 10,000 people, he made the first presidential speech to the NAACP. All Americans were entitled to full civil rights and freedom, he said.

> When I say all Americans, I mean all Americans. Many of our people still suffer the indignity of insults, ... and, I regret to say, the threat of physi-cal and mob violence. Prejudice and intolerance in which these evils are rooted still exist. The conscience of our nation, and the legal machinery
> 5 which enforces it, have not yet secured to each citizen freedom from fear. We cannot wait another decade or another generation to remedy these evils. We must work, as never before, to cure them now.... [We have] reached a turning point in the long history of our country's efforts to guarantee freedom and equality to all our citizens. Each man must be
> 10 guaranteed equality of opportunity. The only limits to an American's achievement should be his ability, his industry and his character.[8]

He urged an end to lynching, the poll tax, and inequality in edu-cation and employment. Walter White felt that for its bravery and in the context of the time, it ranked as one of the greatest presidential speeches. It had been the strongest presidential statement on civil rights since Lincoln himself.

Harry Truman could be as cynical as any man could when votes were at stake but he was also a genuine patriot. He was motivated by the desire to do what was best for America. He wanted American society to retain respect for the law. He felt equality was vital to maintain America's moral standing in the Cold War world. He told black Democrats that better education for blacks would benefit the economy and thereby help all Americans. It was a combination of the black vote, respect for the law, humane revulsion at racist attacks, personal integrity and his perception of what was best for his country that served to turn Truman toward advocacy of greater equality for blacks.

4 Conclusions about Progress under Truman

> **KEY ISSUE** Who or what was most responsible for progress in civil rights in the Truman years?

Clearly, some progress had been made during Truman's presidency. At the very least there was increased awareness of the need for greater equality, and there had been a few concrete advances, such as FEPC and decreased discrimination in federal employment and contracts.

Was it all due to Truman? It is possible that Truman would not have acted as he did without pressure from politicians such as Flynn within his own party, and from black individuals such as Randolph and organisations such as the NAACP and CORE. CORE organised sit-ins and 'Freedom Rides' such as the 1947 'Journey of Reconciliation' through border states, which tried to ensure the enforcement of the Supreme Court ruling against segregation on interstate bus transportation. NAACP used a variety of tactics, such as economic boycotts. For example, in New Orleans in 1947, NAACP activists picketed stores that refused to allow black women to try on hats. The NAACP lawyers were working against 'separate but equal' in the law courts and gained some successes. In 1950 the Supreme Court made three civil rights decisions that set important precedents for future years. It held that segregation on railway dining cars was illegal under the Interstate Commerce Act (HENDERSON v. US), that a black student could not be physically separated from white students in the University of Oklahoma (McLAURIN v. OKLAHOMA STATE REGENTS), and that a separate black Texan law school was not equal to the University of Texas Law School to which the black petitioner had therefore to be admitted (SWEATT v. PAINTER). PLESSY v. FERGUSON was thus almost overturned. In the dying days of Truman's presidency, the administration intervened pro-the plaintiff in BROWN v. BOARD OF EDUCATION OF TOPEKA, which proved vital in the Supreme Court reversal of the separate but equal doctrine in 1954. Local government also played its part. By 1952, 11 states and

20 cities had fair employment laws, 19 states had legislation against some form of racial discrimination, and only five states retained the poll tax. Truman had led by example and his support played a part in attaining all this.

Organisations, institutions, and individuals were responsible for both progress and the lack of it. Congress, dominated by Republicans, refused to pass meaningful civil rights legislation, and hampered a fairer distribution of federal funds to black schools. Truman usually had to resort to Executive Orders to make progress on equality. Public opinion slowed down progress on civil rights. Given the degree of opposition amongst the white electorate and politicians, one must conclude that Truman played a brave and crucial individual role in precipitating change. Americans needed the presidential authority and prestige to move faster on the road to racial equality. Responsibility for the raising of awareness that precipitated presidential and legal actions also lay with the black activists themselves, particularly the trade unionist Randolph and the NAACP.

5 The Eisenhower Years (1952–61)

> **KEY ISSUES** What progress was made toward racial equality in these years? Did President Eisenhower, organisations, institutions, individuals, laws or important events contribute most?

a) The Role of Eisenhower

The Republican President Dwight D. Eisenhower was far less inclined than Truman was to propel America toward racial equality. Why? It was partly his background. He often reminded people he was born in an all-white town in the South and spent much of his life in Southern states and in the segregated armed forces. He shared the typical white fears of miscegenation, assuring his speech writer that his public calls for equality of opportunity did not mean black and white had 'to mingle socially – or that a Negro could court my daughter'. He said he feared the 'great emotional strains' which would arise from desegregating schools. He was ideologically opposed to large-scale federal intervention in any great issue, which was why he rejected the re-establishment of the FEPC. There were also good political reasons for inactivity. His Republican Party had seen the damage inflicted on the Democrats by disagreements over civil rights. The Republicans had done unusually well in the Southern states as a result. The Republican Party could only lose by adopting a firm civil rights platform.

The sole black on Eisenhower's staff, E. Frederic Morrow, was employed in 1955 with the black vote in the presidential election in mind. Initially he arranged parking spaces for staffers, then he answered correspondence from blacks. White House clerks and typists refused to file or type for him and Eisenhower never consulted him on civil rights. Morrow was shocked by the administration's ignorance and concluded that Eisenhower never understood how blacks felt. Eisenhower only met black leaders (King, Wilkins and Randolph) once. Randolph criticised Eisenhower's inactivity and called for more presidential leadership. Eisenhower avoided talking to black Republican Congressman Adam Clayton Powell, whom he considered to be a demagogue. When Powell tried to make federal aid for school-building contingent upon desegregation, that lost the federal aid, which infuriated Eisenhower. Eisenhower's staff felt black organisations over-dramatised incidents of racial injustice, demanded too much time and attention, and were insufficiently grateful for the administration's deeds on their behalf. One presidential aide felt black demands were made with 'ugliness and surliness'.

Eisenhower's lack of leadership is well illustrated in the cases of Emmett Till and Autherine Lucy. In August 1955, Till's mutilated body was dragged out of a Mississippi river. He had been accused of whistling at a white woman. The defence argued that Till was really alive and well in Chicago and that this was all an NAACP plot! The defence lawyer and his congressman brother were leading Democrats in the county. In his appeal to the jurors the lawyer said he was 'sure that every last Anglo-Saxon one of us has the courage to free' the white men accused of the murder. The verdict was 'not guilty'. As late as the 1990s, a Mississippi Democrat claimed Till was deservedly killed because he failed to obey Southern customs. Eisenhower made no comment, in sharp contrast to Truman's brave and just condemnation of the murder of black soldiers. Although Eisenhower always said he would support federal court orders, he also kept quiet about the expulsion of the first black student from the University of Alabama. Autherine Lucy successfully took the University to a federal court to obtain admission, but the University then expelled her. They said she had lied when she claimed she had been excluded because of her race. Eisenhower also refused to give federal support for the Montgomery bus boycott (see page 68).

Eisenhower seemed to hope that race relations would somehow gradually improve of their own accord. He feared that 'if we attempt merely by passing a lot of laws to force someone to like someone else, we are just going to get into trouble'.[9] So, did Eisenhower do anything helpful? In his first State of the Union address (February 1953) he called for a combination of publicity, persuasion and conscience to help end racial discrimination. He reaffirmed Truman's commitment to desegregation of the military, although blacks still did not get equality in promotions or assignments. He also worked against discrimination in federal facilities in Washington and federal hiring, but his President's Committee on Government Contracts lacked teeth.

Although Eisenhower neither aimed nor wanted to do anything

significant to alleviate black problems, he inadvertently managed to do so. How? He rewarded several liberal Southern Republicans with appointment to the Supreme Court. Earl Warren was made a Supreme Court judge as a reward for his support in the 1952 campaign. In BROWN v. THE BOARD OF EDUCATION, TOPEKA, KANSAS (1954) Warren's Supreme Court struck a great blow against segregated schools, despite Eisenhower's opposition. Eisenhower told Warren Southerners were not 'bad people':

> All they are concerned about is to see that their sweet little girls are not required to sit in school alongside some big overgrown Negroes.[10]

Eisenhower refused to use federal power to enforce the BROWN decision, until forced by events at Little Rock, Arkansas (see pages 70–72). His initial silence over BROWN owed much to his belief in the separation of the powers of the president and the judiciary. He disliked federal intrusion into private lives and he feared that some schools would close rather than let in blacks:

> It is all very well to talk about school integration, but you may also be talking about social disintegration. We cannot demand perfection in these moral questions. All we can do is keep working toward a goal.[11]

His public silence was widely interpreted as signifying his lack of support for BROWN. He was relieved when BROWN II (see page 67) set no date for desegregation; this suited his gradualist approach. He refused to condemn the pro-segregation Southern Manifesto (see page 67), saying change would have to be gradual. Eisenhower's speechwriter Arthur Larsen summed it up:

> From all this there emerges the inescapable conclusion that President Eisenhower ... was neither emotionally nor intellectually in favour of combating segregation.[12]

Chief Justice Warren thought that a word of approval from Eisenhower on BROWN would have facilitated a smoother, easier and quicker move toward racial equality. Eisenhower's biographer Stephen Ambrose concluded that until Little Rock, in 1957, Eisenhower provided 'almost no leadership at all' on the most fundamental social and moral problem of his time.[13] On the other hand, Eisenhower supporters claim that his evolutionary approach to civil rights was best for national unity. Eisenhower loved to quote a story he heard while golfing in Augusta, Georgia. An agricultural worker supposedly said, 'If someone does not shut up around here, particularly those Negroes from the North, they are going to get a lot of us niggers killed!'. At least it can be claimed that the civil rights movement did not go backwards during the Eisenhower administration, thanks to the Supreme Court (pages 67–68), events in Montgomery (pages 68–70) and Little Rock (pages 70–72), and also the Civil Rights Acts (page 72).

b) BROWN – 1954

Oliver Brown decided to challenge segregated schools in Topeka, Kansas. Brown could not send his daughter to a whites-only school five blocks away, only to an all-black school 20 blocks away. The NAACP had been working against segregated schools in the law courts, slowly eroding the 'separate but equal' decision of the Supreme Court (PLESSY v. FERGUSON). Now, the NAACP decided to support Brown in his appeal to the Supreme Court. The organisation felt they had a good chance of success, because Kansas was not a Southern state. The leading NAACP lawyer Thurgood Marshall represented Brown before the Supreme Court. Marshall argued that segregation was against the Fourteenth Amendment. Chief Justice Earl Warren believed that even if facilities were equal, separate education was psychologically harmful to black children. The Supreme Court agreed, in defiance of President Eisenhower's wishes. This BROWN ruling was highly significant. It was a great triumph for the NAACP's long campaign against segregated education in the law courts. BROWN seemed to remove all constitutional sanction for racial segregation by overturning PLESSY v. FERGUSON. However, the victory was not total: the Supreme Court did nothing to set standards in schools, and gave no date by which desegregation had to be achieved. The NAACP returned to the Supreme Court in BROWN II (1955) to obtain the ruling that integration be accomplished 'with all deliberate speed', but there was still no date for compliance. Warren believed schools and administrators needed time to adjust. The white reaction suggests that Warren was right. White Citizens Councils were quickly formed throughout the South to defend segregation. By 1956 they boasted around a quarter of a million members. The Councils challenged desegregation plans in the law courts. Some school boards maintained white-only schools by manipulating entry criteria. There was a 'massive resistance' campaign in Virginia, and some schools were closed. Virginia labour unions financed segregated schools when the public schools were closed. Acceptance of the BROWN ruling varied. In the peripheral and urban South desegregation was introduced quite quickly, as in Washington DC and some towns and cities in Maryland, Virginia, Texas, Arkansas, North Carolina, Tennessee and Florida. Reluctant whites therein accepted the law of the land, unlike whites in the heart of the old Confederacy, in Georgia, South Carolina, Alabama, Mississippi, and Louisiana. BROWN now became a central issue in Southern politics. With three exceptions, Southern politicians signed the Southern Manifesto. The signatories committed themselves to fight against the BROWN decision, and thereby the Supreme Court! President Eisenhower said the federal government had no power to intervene when his political ally the governor of Texas used state troopers to prevent school integration. It was the incident at Little Rock, Arkansas, precipitated by the Supreme Court decision, which forced Eisenhower's hand (see below, pages 70–72).

c) The Montgomery Bus Boycott (1956)

The Montgomery Bus Boycott is seen by many as the real start of the American civil rights movement. It all began in December 1955. Mrs Rosa Parks returned home by bus after a hard day's work as a seamstress in a department store in Montgomery, Alabama. The bus soon filled up. A white man was left standing. The bus driver ordered her and three other blacks to move because of the city ordinance that said no black could sit parallel with a white passenger. The others moved, but Mrs Parks refused. She was arrested, and charged with a violation of the Montgomery city bus segregation ordinance.

Many writers portray 42 year-old Rosa Parks as a tired old lady who had been exhausted by the day at work and could not take any more. But her defiance was not unpremeditated. She had joined the NAACP in 1943. She soon became Montgomery branch secretary. The branch had been looking to challenge Montgomery's bus segregation laws. They had contemplated using Claudette Colvin who had been arrested in March 1955 for refusing to give up a seat to a white passenger. But Colvin was a pregnant, unmarried teenager who was also accused of assault. Rosa Parks provided a far better test case. Once she had been arrested, the NAACP and (black) Alabama State College helped her. Students copied and distributed propaganda leaflets to elicit total support from the black community. Believing that church involvement would increase working class black participation and decrease the possibility of disorder, NAACP worked with local church leaders, especially Dr Martin Luther King Jr. The 26-year old Baptist minister had already rejected an offer to lead the local NAACP branch, but he let his church be used as a meeting place to plan a bus boycott to protest at Parks' arrest. The church would thus provide the organisation, location, inspiration, and some financial aid.

Boycotts hit white pockets and were an old and effective mass weapon. Blacks had boycotted streetcars throughout the South from 1900–6. In March 1953, blacks in Baton Rouge, Louisiana, used their economic power (most bus passengers were black) to gain bus seating on a first-come-first-served basis. These Baton Rouge tactics were now adopted by Martin Luther King in Montgomery. Thus the Montgomery bus boycott had its origins in grass-roots black activism and in two well-established black organisations, NAACP and the church. Blacks successfully boycotted Montgomery buses on the day of Rosa Parks' trial. Blacks demanded the bus company use a first-come-first-served system, that drivers should be polite to blacks, and that black drivers be employed. No-one as yet demanded an end to segregation on the buses. The city commissioners rejected the proposed changes so the one-day boycott became a year-long one. The community agreed that King would be a good leader of the boycott. Why? Some historians say he was a compromise candidate, others that there was no better alternative. The NAACP lacked the influence of the church, while Alabama State College employees risked dismissal. King therefore headed the new umbrella organisation, the Montgomery Improvement Association (MIA).

The Montgomery White Citizens Council organised the opposition. Its membership doubled from 6000 in February 1956 to 12,000 by March. The Council was dominated by leading city officials who ordered harassment of blacks. King was arrested for the first time (January 1956). He had done 30-mph in a 25-mph zone. On 30 January his house was bombed. His family urged him to quit. He said later he was tempted but felt called by God to continue. King's speeches were inspirational and even appealed to some whites:

> If we are wrong, the Supreme Court of this nation is wrong. If we are wrong, the Constitution of the United States is wrong. If we are wrong, Jesus of Nazareth was merely a ... dreamer.[14]

He stressed this was 'non-violent protest', but it was not 'passive resistance', it was 'active non-violent resistance to evil'.

Montgomery whites used Alabama's anti-boycott law against the black community, and their mass indictments attracted national media coverage. Northerners made collections for Montgomery blacks. King was the first boycott leader to be tried. He was found guilty, and given the choice of a fine or 368 days in jail. This white hostility made the MIA up the stakes. In a case partly funded by the NAACP in June the federal district court said segregation on buses was unconstitutional (BROWDER v. GAYLE). It cited BROWN (see page 67). Montgomery city commissioners appealed to the Supreme Court but the Supreme Court backed the federal district court. The boycott was called off when desegregated buses began operating (December 1956). The Ku Klux Klan responded by sending 40 carloads of robed and hooded members through Montgomery's 'nigger town'. Blacks did not retreat behind closed doors as usual, but came out and waved at the motorcade!

In Montgomery itself, the boycott was a limited victory. Apart from the buses, the city remained segregated. However, that black reaction to the Ku Klux Klan showed morale had been boosted. This was a small victory with big implications. It did not just happen: it was a result of black organisation (the church and NAACP) that had been developing for years. It copied previous tactics (Baton Rouge). It demonstrated the power of a whole black community using direct but non-violent action. It inspired similar bus boycotts in several Southern communities. It showed the continuing effectiveness of the NAACP strategy of working through the law courts and the importance of dedicated individuals such as Rosa Parks. It demonstrated the importance of the churches in the fight for equality. Ironically it demonstrated how white extremism frequently helped to increase black unity and determination. It revealed the hatred and determined racism of many white Southerners, but also the idealism of a handful of Southern whites like Reverend Robert Graetz, minister at a black Lutheran church in Montgomery, who supported the boycott. His house was bombed. The Montgomery boycott inspired more Northern white support and more co-operation between Northern and Southern blacks. A. Philip Randolph gave financial support. The boycott inspired others, including Melba Pattillo (see below). Perhaps most important of all, it brought King, with all his inspirational rhetorical gifts, to the forefront of the movement (see chapter 5). In 1957 he helped establish a new organisation, the Southern Christian Leadership Conference (SCLC). This proved to be particularly important at a time when NAACP was being persecuted in the Deep South.

d) Little Rock

Governor Orville Faubus of Arkansas was struggling to get re-elected. He decided to exploit white racism to ensure re-election. The city of Little Rock's plans for compliance with BROWN were scheduled to come to slow completion in 1963. However, nine black students reported to Central High School in September 1957. Faubus declared that it was his duty to prevent the disorder that would arise from integration. He ordered the National Guard to surround the school and to keep black students out.

One of the nine students, Melba Pattillo, wrote about her experiences years later. She had volunteered to be a 'guinea pig' when asked by the NAACP and church leaders. Her father was against it, saying it endangered her and his job. A white man violently assaulted her crying, 'I'll show you niggers the Supreme Court cannot run my life'. Others cried, 'Keep away from our school', 'Go back to the jungle', 'Lynch the niggers'. She was inspired by the 'self-assured air' of Thurgood Marshall, and had the backing of her mother and grandmother, many blacks and a few whites. A white boy, whom she trusted despite the warnings of her family, befriended Melba at Central High. Subsequently though, she 'wonder [ed] what possessed my parents and the adults of the NAACP to allow us to go to school in the face of such violence'.[15]

Eisenhower had said before the crisis that he could never envisage sending in federal troops to enforce the federal court ruling (which had doubtless encouraged Faubus). However, Little Rock's mayor now told Eisenhower the mob was out of hand, so Eisenhower sent in troops to protect the black children. While Southerners cried 'Invasion!', Eisenhower's radio speech to the nation tried to restore harmony. He said he had acted because of his 'inescapable' responsibility for enforcing the law. He made no mention of integration. He blamed 'disorderly mobs' and 'demagogic extremists'. He again

A black student tries to enter Central High School, in Little Rock, Arkansas, despite the hostility shown by the white crowd.

refused to endorse BROWN, and tried to rally the nation by saying its Soviet enemies were making propaganda capital out of Little Rock. He stressed that most Southerners were law-abiding.

Why had the great opponent of federal intervention intervened? Eisenhower had tried but failed to negotiate a settlement with Faubus. His public appeals to the rioters had been ignored. Local officials had begged him to act. The Constitution and federal law seemed threatened. Finally, Eisenhower was concerned about America's international 'prestige and influence'.

How significant was Little Rock? It showed that Supreme Court rulings like BROWN met tremendous grass-roots resistance in practice. Blacks tried to push things along faster at Little Rock, and still there was no dramatic immediate improvement. Neither local nor national authorities were keen to enforce BROWN. Faubus did what Eisenhower had always feared and closed the schools rather than integrate. Eisenhower did not respond. It was 1960 before Central High was integrated. Only 2–3% of America's black children attended de-segregated schools as late as 1964. However, the image of black children being harassed and spat at by aggressive white adults in Little Rock was a brilliant propaganda victory for the NAACP. It helped to influence moderate white opinion. The Supreme Court ploughed ahead. In

COOPER v. AARON (1958) it said any law ('ingenious or ingenuous') which sought to keep public schools segregated was unconstitutional. Finally, and perhaps most significantly, blacks realised that they probably needed to do more than rely on court decisions.

e) Eisenhower's Civil Rights Acts

In order to win the black vote in the 1956 election year, the Eisenhower administration drew up a civil rights bill. The bill aimed to ensure all citizens could exercise the right to vote (only 20% of Southern blacks were registered voters as yet). It proposed a new Justice Department division to monitor such civil rights abuses, and a bipartisan civil rights commission report on race relations. In his State of the Union address in January 1957, Eisenhower praised the bill. He expressed 'shock' that only 7000 of Mississippi's 900,000 blacks were allowed to vote, and that registrars were setting impossible questions (such as 'How many bubbles are there in a bar of soap?') for blacks trying to register.

Democratic senators worked to weaken the bill. They thought it would damage national and party unity. They claimed it sought to use federal power 'to force a co-mingling of white and Negro children'. Eisenhower then cravenly claimed he did not really know what was in the bill ('there were certain phrases I did not completely understand') and did not fight to keep it intact. Strom Thurmond filibustered for 24 hours to try to kill the bill. It passed into a much-weakened act which did little to help blacks exercise the vote, as any public official indicted for obstructing a black voter would be tried by an all-white jury. As the first such act since Reconstruction, it pleased some black leaders. Others felt it was a nauseating sham.

In late 1958, Eisenhower introduced another bill because he was concerned about bombings of black schools and churches. While Eisenhower considered the bill to be moderate, Southern Democrats again diluted its provisions. It finally became law because both parties sought the black vote in the presidential election year. The act established penalties for obstructing black exercise of the franchise. These Civil Rights Acts of 1957 and 1960 only added 3% of black voters to the electoral roles during 1960. 'Essentially', says Ambrose, Eisenhower 'passed on to his successors the problem of guaranteeing constitutional rights to Negro citizens'.[16] Contemporaries were also unimpressed, but at least the acts acknowledged federal responsibilities and thereby encouraged civil rights activists to work for more legislation.

f) The Cold War and Colonialism

Apparently unrelated events such as the Cold War and decolonisation sometimes impacted upon the progress of racial equality.

The need for national unity during America's Cold War with

Communist Russia helps explain Eisenhower's frequent inactivity on civil rights. He did not want to antagonise America's white majority. Black civil rights activists with Communist sympathies became very unpopular, especially amongst trade unionists who wanted to prove their patriotism. The Cold War thus damaged the civil rights–labour axis. However, the Cold War helped as well as hindered the civil rights movement. It was difficult for both Truman and Eisenhower to try to rally the free world against Communist totalitarianism when blacks in the American South were so clearly unfree. It is probably no coincidence that the Hungarian uprising against Soviet oppression (1956) and Britain's granting of independence to Ghana were followed by the Civil Rights Act in America. Significantly, Thurgood Marshall acted as legal adviser to Kenyan nationalists seeking independence from Britain. Decolonisation inspired black Americans such as Melba Pattillo, whose grandmother told her to read about Gandhi's struggle for independence from British colonialism.

g) Conclusions

The historian Robert Cook sees 'relative federal inactivity' and 'limited organisational goals' as the main reason why the civil rights movement stood relatively still in the late 1950s.[17] It was blacks themselves who bore greatest responsibility for precipitating such change as there was in the Eisenhower years. Activists, especially the NAACP, were the moving force behind the Supreme Court decisions, Little Rock and the Montgomery bus boycott. This incessant black pressure along with the international situation and the black vote, forced the Eisenhower administration to propose civil rights legislation.

Although the Supreme Court had declared segregated schools unconstitutional (BROWN), desegregation proved painfully slow. This was due to a powerful white backlash. In 1960, only 6.4% of blacks went to integrated schools in the South, and only 2% in the Deep South. On the other hand, BROWN could be considered as the first breach in the dam, which ensured further progress. Many historians talk of a 20 year 'Second Reconstruction' dating from BROWN.

Eisenhower's Civil Rights Acts were so weak as to be dismissed by many blacks as irrelevant. Others however felt they were another breach in the dam. Unlike Truman, Eisenhower did not seem to want to give much help the black movement toward equality. However, others forced his hand, as at Little Rock.

The civil rights movement was acquiring 'heroes', such as Rosa Parks. However, there were also victims such as Emmett Till. There were signs that mass action could bring about results, as in the Montgomery bus boycott, but this was still not a universal, organised movement. There was no single, strong black organisation. After BROWN the NAACP was persecuted in the South, and was jealous of the emerging SCLC. NAACP met some great setbacks, such as obstructive federal judges and unsuccessful attempts at mass action. King's Crusade for Citizenship failed because as yet SCLC lacked the massive grass-roots support and organisational infrastructure necessary for success. Progress on voting rights awaited greater federal assistance against recalcitrant Southern states, and the mobilisation of rural blacks.

INDIANS – A COMPARATIVE STUDY

ISSUES

How does the history of the Indians in the 1950s compare and contrast with that of blacks? Why were there similarities and differences?

The historian Angie Debo described the 1950s as 'back to the bad old days'.[18] Commissioner Dillon Myer (1950) reversed Collier's policies (see pages 44–45). Myer intervened in tribal affairs in dictatorial fashion, for example, selling Pueblo Indian land without their consent. He wanted to break-up Indian reservations and scatter the people. Myer's relocation programme aimed to get Indians jobs in the cities, but one third of Indians returned to their reservations, and those who remained in the cities often ended up on welfare. Indians felt Myer was trying to destroy Indian civilisation. They wanted jobs to be brought to reservations. Congress also disliked tribal self-government. They 'terminated' some reservations, usually where the Indians were few, poor, and on land that might prove valuable to white men. Scattered bands of poor, illiterate Utah Paiutes were 'terminated' because it was believed there was oil and uranium on their land. Congress aimed to save the white taxpayer subsidising Indians, and to release Indian lands for white economic development. In 1953 Congress increased state government jurisdiction over reservations. A good example of the unsympathetic attitude of state authorities is the state of Vermont's sterilisation of disproportionate numbers of Indians because they were supposedly 'immoral', 'criminal', or 'suspected feeble-minded'.[19]

Thus Indians, like blacks, found federal and state government unsympathetic in the 1950s. However, while blacks still made some progress toward equality, Indians did not. Why? Blacks had more contact with whites, so they used white traditions such as national organisation and litigation. Indians on the other hand were fewer in number, less urbanised, and culturally disorientated. Separate tribes and geographical segregation militated against national and effective organisations. Therefore, Indians were easier prey for an administration that preached the virtues of self-help and minimal federal intervention.

References

1 Quoted in David McCullough, *Truman*, New York, 1992, p. 54.
2 Ibid., p. 86.
3 Ibid., p. 247.
4 Ibid., p. 297.
5 Ibid., p. 639.
6 Ibid., pp. 586–9.
7 Quoted in Alonso Hamby, *Man of the People*, Oxford, 1995, p. 433.
8 Quoted in McCullough, p. 570, and Hamby, p. 366.
9 Quoted in C.J. Pach and E. Richardson, *The Presidency of Dwight D. Eisenhower*, Kansas, 1991, p. 142.
10 Quoted in Stephen Ambrose, *Eisenhower: Soldier and President*, Simon and Schuster, 1990, p. 367. Equally reputable historians, Pach and Richardson, p. 142, quote Eisenhower as saying ' big sexually advanced black boys'.
11 Pach and Richardson, p. 143.
12 Ibid., p. 157.
13 Ambrose, p. 368.
14 Quoted in Stephen Oates, *Let the Trumpet Sound: A Life of Martin Luther King*, Cannongate Books, 1994, p. 71.
15 Quoted in W.T.M. Riches, *The Civil Rights Movement*, Macmillan, 1997, pp. 27–8.
16 Ambrose, p. 445.
17 Robert Cook, *Sweet Land of Liberty?*, Longman, 1998, p. 107.
18 Angie Debo, *A History of the Indians of the United States*, Pimlico, 1995, p. 350.
19 Nancy Gallagher, *Breeding Better Vermonters*, Vermont, 1999.

Summary Diagram

Who/ What helped progress (1945–60)?	Who/ What hindered progress (1945–60)?
Truman	Truman
Eisenhower	Eisenhower
Congress	Congress
The Supreme Court	The Supreme Court
The judiciary	The judiciary
Churches	
Biracial and black organisations	White supremacist organisations
Ordinary people, especially blacks	Ordinary people, especially whites
Cold War	Cold War
Decolonisation	

Working on Chapter 4

To clarify your thoughts on who and what helped and hindered black progress 1945–60, you could:

1 Pick out signs of progress, for example, 'To Secure These Rights', BROWN, the Montgomery Bus Boycott, civil rights legislation, and Little Rock.
2 Note the significance of those signs – did they change things overnight or were they limited successes?
3 Look at all the individuals and institutions contributing to those landmarks. A pattern might then emerge to help you decide the most important factor.

Answering structured and essay questions on Chapter 4

Think about these questions:

a) In what ways did Truman help blacks? (*8 marks*)
b) In what ways did Eisenhower help blacks? (*8 marks*)
c) Who did more for blacks, Truman or Eisenhower? (*14 marks*)

The above structured questions are a useful reminder that what structured questions do is to structure a potentially longer essay for you. So, when you come to full essay questions, you can feel confident – you have done at all before.

Think about this question: 'How important was the Supreme Court in the black struggle for equality 1945–60?' It is important to weigh up the words very carefully. 'How important' suggests you need to consider the importance of other factors, for example, the presidents and other important individuals, organisations, Congress, and public opinion. Imagine this was a structured question, and break it down into three parts: What did the Supreme Court do to help blacks? How important was that help? How important were other factors in comparison?

In the last part of your essay (the third part) you need to compare other factors continually with the Supreme Court, for example, while stressing the importance of BROWN, you would also recognise the significance of the NAACP involvement.

Answering source-based questions on Chapter 4

Look at the source extracts on pages 56, 57, 59, 60, 62, 65, 66, 69. Think about the following questions:

a) Explain the following references:
   i) 'we are 172 years too late' (page 60)
   ii) 'my inclination as a native of Missouri' (page 62) (*2 marks*)
b) How do Truman (pages 57, 62) and Eisenhower (page 65) disagree on the issue of equality before the law? (*3 marks*)
c) How reliable a guide are Truman's public utterances (pages 57, 62) to his attitude to black people? (*3 marks*)
d) Suggest reasons why the historians attribute different words to Eisenhower. (pages 66, 75) (*3 marks*)
e) Using the sources and your own knowledge, what sort of arguments were being given for and against the granting of equality to American blacks? (*9 marks*)

Remember, source questions require you to have detailed factual knowledge.

5 King or Knave?

POINTS TO CONSIDER

The years 1956–68 saw much civil rights activity and some dramatic black gains. This chapter looks at the extent to which Martin Luther King was responsible for them. Did this one man make the movement or did the movement make him? The chapter investigates King's organisational skills, the quality of his campaign strategy and tactics, his saintly reputation and also assesses his achievements. Readers will form their own opinions.

KEY DATES

1955 King involved in the Montgomery bus boycott.
1956 Supreme Court declared segregation on buses unconstitutional.
1957 Southern Christian Leadership Conference (SCLC) formed.
Desegregation crisis at Little Rock. Civil Rights Act.
1960 Anti-segregation Sit-ins began in the South.
1961 Anti-segregation Freedom Riders travelled the South. Albany Movement.
1963 Birmingham riots. March on Washington.
1964 Civil Rights Act.
1965 Selma to Montgomery march. Voting Rights Act.
1966 Watts (black Los Angeles ghetto) riots. King focused on ghettos.
1966 'Black power' dominated 'Meredith March' (Mississippi).
1967 Northern ghetto race riots.
1968 King assassinated.

Martin Luther King is one of America's most controversial figures. Contemporaries were bitterly divided in their assessment of him. Many whites considered him a Communist or a rabble-rouser, who provoked violence and disorder in American cities. Towards the end of his life, many blacks considered him to be an ineffectual 'Uncle Tom'. Other contemporaries, black and white, admired him greatly. After his death, King became an inspirational and perhaps unrealistically saintly figure to many throughout the world.

Historians differ in their assessment of King's importance in the civil rights movement. Professor Clayborne Carson contends that

> If King had never lived, the black struggle would have followed a course of development similar to the one it did. The Montgomery bus boycott would have occurred, because King did not initiate it. Black students ... had sources of tactical and ideological inspiration besides King.[1]

Professor Anthony Badger disagrees, believing that there was a 'revolution in Southern race relations' due to the civil rights movement, in which 'no person was more important' than King.[2] Historians also disagree about the strengths and weaknesses of King as an organizer and visionary within the civil rights movement.

This chapter looks at how King's career illuminates race relations and the struggle for equality in the United States, and at the debates about King's strengths, weaknesses, achievements and failures.

1 The Life and Career of Martin Luther King Jr. (1929–68)

KEY ISSUE How do King's life and career illustrate twentieth century American race relations?

King's grandfather was founder and pastor of a Baptist church in Atlanta, Georgia. King's father inherited the pastorate. Both were NAACP activists. King was thus born into a well-educated and relatively prosperous family who knew how the church and NAACP strengthened the black community.

As a small child, King had a white friend. The boys had to attend separate schools. Then, King recalled:

> He told me that one day his father had demanded that he would play with me no more. I never will forget what a great shock this was to me. ... For the first time, I was made aware of the existence of a race problem.[3]

If young Martin wanted 'a day out' downtown, he would have to travel at the back of the bus. He could not buy a soda or hot dog at a downtown store lunch counter. If a white drugstore served him, they would hand him his ice cream through a side window and in a paper cup so no white would ever have to use any plate that he had used. He had to drink from the 'colored' water fountain, and use the 'colored' restroom. He had to sit in the 'colored' section at the back of the balcony in the movie theatre. Then he had to return to 'nigger town'. King said it made him 'determined to hate every white person'.

King received poor quality education in Atlanta's segregated schools then went North to college, where he experienced further racial prejudice. A Philadelphia restaurant refused to serve him. When he demanded service, his plate arrived filled with sand. A New Jersey restaurant owner drew a gun on King when he refused to leave. King had problems getting student accommodation in Boston (1951):

> I went into place after place where there were signs that rooms were for rent. They were for rent until they found out I was a Negro and suddenly they had just been rented.[4]

However, his attitude to whites had changed. He particularly liked white women, and was devastated when friends convinced him that marriage to a white sweetheart would not work. Instead he married fellow black student Coretta Scott. She hated the segregated South, but King insisted on returning there, 'because that's where I'm needed'.

Initially King had not wanted to be a minister; he said the church concentrated on life in the next world instead of working to improve life in this world. However, he felt called by God to serve humanity and became pastor of a 'rich folks church' in Montgomery, Alabama (1954). King urged his congregation to register to vote and join the NAACP. His involvement in the black boycott of Montgomery's segregated buses (see pages 85–86) resulted in many threats on his life and family. His family urged him to give up activism. He wavered, but

> it seemed at that moment that I could hear an inner voice saying to me, 'Martin Luther, stand-up for righteousness. Stand-up for justice. Stand-up for truth. And lo I will be with you, even until the end of the world' ... I heard the voice of Jesus.... He promised never to leave me.[5]

The threat of violence was unceasing but did not deter King. 'My cause, my race, is worth dying for,' he said. He lacked reliable legal protection down South. Soon after the bus boycott, two whites who had confessed to trying to blow up King's home were adjudged innocent by an all-white Alabama jury. He was nearly killed on a 1958 visit to Harlem. A deranged black woman stabbed him. It took hours for surgeons to remove the blade, which was millimetres from his aorta. Had King sneezed while awaiting the blade's removal, he would have died.

By 1958 King had helped establish the SCLC (Southern Christian Leadership Conference) which aimed to gain greater equality for American blacks, and he was recognised as one of black America's leading spokesmen. He had the first of several White House meetings.

In January 1960 King moved to Atlanta, Georgia, because SCLC had its headquarters there. Atlanta's race relations were as bad as Montgomery's. The restaurant in SCLC's office building refused to serve King. He said his small daughter found it hard to understand why she could not have an ice cream there.

Few blacks were registered to vote in the segregated South, so blacks lacked the political power to change the situation. King therefore became increasingly involved in demonstrations to draw attention to black problems, such as 'sit-ins' in segregated Southern restaurants (1960) and protests against segregated public facilities in Albany, Georgia, and Birmingham, Alabama (1961–2). Although he always stressed that demonstrations should be peaceful and non-violent he was frequently arrested participating in them. The resultant publicity usually led to progress, as when the Supreme Court declared Birmingham's segregation laws unconstitutional (1963).

King drew national and international attention to black problems. As one of the leaders of a large, integrated March on Washington, he made the brilliant and inspirational 'I have a dream' speech (1963) (see page 94). In 1964 he received the Nobel Peace Prize in Norway. In 1965 King was involved in a great protest march in Alabama. His actions encouraged President Johnson to obtain civil rights legislation. King then concentrated on the problems of Northern black ghettos. His workload was heavy. On one hot July weekend in Chicago in 1965, he made 20 speeches in less than 48 hours. The workload, the constant fear for his life, the slow rate of progress, ghetto riots and increasing numbers of black and white extremists, all made him increasingly pessimistic.

King's pessimism encompassed blacks and whites. 'The vast majority of white Americans are racist,' he said. He felt 'hypocritical' white Americans never intended to share 'democracy' with blacks. Whites had committed a kind of 'psychological and spiritual genocide' against blacks. When riots broke out in the black ghettos in the hot summer of 1967, King blamed Congress for having failed to alleviate black poverty. In Newark, New Jersey, 23 died and 725 were injured. When NAACP leader Roy Wilkins condemned the rioters, King described him to Coretta as 'hopeless', lacking any 'integrity or philosophy'. His impatience was not confined to black moderates like Wilkins. He was exasperated by militant black racists like Stokely Carmichael. 'Many people who would otherwise be ashamed of their anti-Negro feeling now have an excuse.' However, 'Stokely is not the problem. The problem is white people and their attitude.'

Towards the end of his life, whites and blacks became increasingly critical of him. When he toured riot-stricken Cleveland, Ohio, some black teenagers mocked and ignored him. Many blacks considered him to be too moderate, an 'Uncle Tom' who was in awe of white authority figures. Many whites considered him to be an extremist. The *Washington Post* accused King of inciting anarchy because he had threatened to bring Washington to a standstill, saying,

> We've got to find a method that will disrupt our cities if necessary, create the crisis that will force the nation to look at the situation, dramatise it, and yet at the same time not destroy life or property ... I see that as massive civil disobedience.[6]

He felt he had overestimated the successes of 1955–65 and underestimated black rage and white bigotry. He recognised that his failure to overcome that resistance had made him unpopular amongst blacks:

> 1   When hope diminishes the hate element is often turned toward those who originally built up the hope. The bitterness is often greater toward that person who built up the hope, who could say 'I have a dream,' but couldn't produce the dream because of the failure and the sickness of
> 5   the nation to respond to the dream.[7]

In spring 1968 King went to support black strikers in Memphis, Tennessee. There, he was assassinated by a social misfit who called him Martin 'Lucifer' King or Martin Luther 'Coon'.

King's early life reflected the prejudice faced by blacks in mid-twentieth century America, but also the help and encouragement to be found in the black church. The story of his activism reads like a history of the civil rights movement. He was involved in most of its significant events, and the hostility he met with, from both blacks and whites, shows how difficult it was to campaign to bring about change at a universally acceptable speed. Some blacks thought he moved too slowly. Some whites thought him too extreme.

2 Saint or Sinner?

KEY ISSUE Does King deserve his saint-like reputation?

King's campaign depended greatly upon convincing people of the morality of the racial equality he sought. Therefore, many people believed that his campaign and his behaviour should be above reproach. His enemies and critics were quick to say that they were not.

King worked hard to counter criticisms that he was a glory seeker. In 1958 a friend criticised his account of the Montgomery bus boycott for giving the impression 'that everything depended on you', King revised it to emphasise the contributions of others. Many of King's actions could be interpreted as either helpful to the black cause or as attention seeking, depending upon one's view of King's motivation. In 1963, for example, a Mississippi NAACP leader was shot. King proposed some joint action but NAACP leader Roy Wilkins felt it was none of King's business. Wilkins told the press that King was presumptuous and self-promoting. According to his friends, King did not want to be famous. They said that while he felt God had called him to leadership, he craved a more normal existence. The problem was that King had to publicise the cause. In 1958, for example, he chose a jail sentence in preference to a $10 fine. Initially he denied it was a 'publicity stunt' but then admitted, 'sometimes it is necessary to dramatise an issue because many people are not aware of what is happening.' King's view was that in order to end the greater evil of inequality, lesser evils had sometimes to be tolerated and even encouraged. When it proved difficult to mobilise sufficient demonstrators in Birmingham (1963), for example, King reluctantly enlisted enthusiastic black high school students, although he knew they were likely to get hurt. 'The press is leaving,' he said. 'You know, we've got to get something going.' Critics accused him of hypocrisy:

He marches for peace on one day, and then the very next day threatens actions we think are coldly calculated to bring violent responses from otherwise peaceful neighbourhoods.[8]

King was sometimes accused of jealousy toward other black leaders. Although usually tolerant of other activists, King clashed with Adam Clayton Powell and Jesse Jackson. When Powell was threatened with the loss of his seat because of what other congressmen called 'inappropriate' behaviour, King said he did not care, because Powell was uncooperative, threatening, too critical of other civil rights leaders, and lacking in personal integrity. Initially, young divinity student Jesse Jackson impressed King. Jackson's 'Operation Breadbasket' helped improve the economic situation of Chicago blacks. Although amazingly charitable toward the foibles and faults of his SCLC workers, King was unconvinced that Jackson was selfless. Opinions of their occasional antagonism varied. Some colleagues believed 'Martin had problems with Jesse because Jesse would ask questions'. Others agreed with King's doubts about Jackson.

Under pressure of events, King was not always truthful. For example, during the troubles in Birmingham, Birmingham businessmen and King both gave distorted versions of their agreement.

King knew his weaknesses. Coretta described her husband as 'a guilt-ridden man', who 'criticised himself more severely than anyone else' did, and felt unworthy of the adulation and acclaim he received. For example, he publicly preached the importance of monogamy and declared sex outside marriage sinful, but privately it was a different matter. One new SCLC worker was shocked to find SCLC headquarters 'very raunchy', and said all of King's intimates had trouble dealing with King's sexuality – 'a saint with clay feet'. The FBI believed King was a national security threat, so they monitored his phone calls and bugged his hotel rooms. They were thrilled to hear King and several SCLC colleagues involved in a drunken party in Washington with two women from Philadelphia. The FBI chief, a homosexual with a fondness for young boys, described King as a 'tom cat' with 'obsessive degenerate sexual urges'. The FBI were disappointed when King and a colleague, on a Hawaiian holiday with two Californian lady friends, produced nothing but the sound of the TV playing loudly – King had guessed he was being bugged. The FBI chief told journalists and church leaders 'off the record' about King's Communist friends and moral degeneracy. The SCLC leadership was concerned about the impact such revelations could have. King's sex life could be used to discredit him and the civil rights movement itself. King was depressed about his romantic affairs, which he considered to be sinful, but could not bring himself to stop. ' I was away from home 25 to 27 days a month,' said King. 'Fucking is a form of anxiety reduction.' King by now had a virtual second wife, but also many one night stands. Some friends considered it just standard pastoral care, common in black churches. 'Everybody was out getting laid,' recalled one activist.

King's fame gave him more opportunities than most. At a New York fundraising party, one observer was fascinated:

1 I watched women making passes at Martin Luther King. I COULD NOT
   BELIEVE what I was seeing in white Westchester [a wealthy commuter
   area] women.... It was unbelievable.... They would walk up to him and
   they would sort of lick their lips and hint and [hand him] notes.... After
5 I saw that thing that evening, I didn't blame him.[9]

Another great criticism of King was that he had a 'Messiah complex' and actually wanted to be a martyr. He always denied that. He certainly lived in fear. In 1964, he walked out on SCLC staffers who wanted him to visit Mississippi where the Ku Klux Klan had vowed to kill him. He returned an hour later to acknowledge that he had to do it. Was he playing to his audience? He was certainly willing to die for a noble cause. He always said his race was dying for, and his willingness to do so is a main reason why many now consider him to be a saintly figure. There are other reasons. He was so un-interested in material gain as to cause great tension with his family. His family considered him careless about his provision for their material well being. He was unconcerned about large houses or insurance policies. When he was awarded the Nobel Peace Prize and $54,000, he rejected Coretta's proposal that he put aside $5000 for each of their children's education. He said the money was for the movement, not him.

King was willing to compromise his popularity for what he believed in. Some SCLC workers hated King's emphasis upon drawing in other economically deprived groups. One complained that a Hispanic 'did not understand that we were the parents and he was the child'. Another said, 'I don't think I am at the point where a Mexican can sit in and call strategy.' King was more than a black civil rights spokesman. 'I am interested in rights for Negroes, but I am just as interested in Appalachian whites and Mexican Americans and other minorities.' His anti-Vietnam war pronouncements were unpopular with many civil rights activists who felt this was alienating President Johnson and damaging their cause. King tried to maintain silence on the war for a while. However, pictures of young Vietnamese children wounded by American firepower, and the knowledge that the war was diverting money from social reform programmes, made King speak out again. 'I know it can hurt SCLC, but I feel better.' He defended his anti-Vietnam speeches by saying, 'I was politically unwise, but morally wise.' Opinion polls showed 73% of Americans disagreed with his opposition to the war, 60% believed his opposition had hurt the civil rights movement, and 48% of blacks thought he was wrong.

His commitment to a public career cost him dear. His domestic life paid a terrible price. He spent relatively little time at home and Coretta felt left out. 'I've never been on the scene when we've marched. I'm usually at home, because my husband says, "You have to take care of the children"'. On one occasion the FBI recorded an exceptionally angry telephone exchange between the neglected Coretta, and her exhausted and pressured husband. On the day that King was in Washington for the signing of the 1964 Civil Rights Act, his two sons were in hospital for tonsilectomies. Coretta was furious when her husband forgot to phone to check on them. Towards the end of King's life, his close friend Reverend Ralph Abernathy was shocked by how King was changing. 'He was just a different person. . . . Sad and depressed.' King paid the ultimate price for his public career when, as he had so often predicted, he was assassinated.

3 How Effective a Leader was King?

> **KEY ISSUES** Did King make the civil rights movement? Or did the movement make King? Was King good at organisation, strategy and tactics? How successful were the events in which he was involved?

Historians disagree over the extent to which King was responsible for protest and progress from 1956 to 1968. In order to assess King's leadership of the movement it is necessary to look at the main events and trends, investigating at each stage the extent to which King was leading or being led, and the wisdom of his strategy and tactics.

a) The Montgomery Bus Boycott

To what extent was King the leader of the Montgomery bus boycott (see pages 68–70)? Local NAACP activists started the protest. King and other churchmen took up the leadership. Blacks throughout America donated money. Montgomery whites could not believe that the boycott was a local movement: 'we know the niggers are not that smart'. However, it was the 50,000 ordinary black people of Montgomery who bore the brunt of the boycott. Local white officials and the bus company also deserve credit! Their stubborn and frequently spiteful reactions inspired ordinary blacks to continue the boycott, even when the church leaders temporarily faltered. Legal costs were borne by the NAACP so it could be argued that NAACP was the single most important factor. The feeling developed that King was the focal point of the boycott, but he said,

> I just happened to be here. . . . If M. L. King had never been born this movement would have taken place . . . there comes a time when time itself is ready for change. That time has come in Montgomery, and I had nothing to do with it.[10]

One local activist agreed: it was 'a protest of the people . . . not a one-man show . . . the leaders couldn't stop it if they wanted to'. King's lieutenant, Reverend Ralph Abernathy, could perhaps as well have fulfilled King's role.

King claimed the boycott signalled the emergence of 'the New Negro', but Roy Wilkins disagreed:

1 The Negro of 1956 who stands on his own two feet is not a new Negro; he is the grandson or the great grandson of the men who hated slavery. By his own hands, through his own struggles, in his own organised groups – of churches, fraternal societies, the NAACP and others –
5 he has fought his way to the place where he now stands.[11]

Wilkins was jealous of King's increasing prominence, keen to emphasise NAACP's importance, and opposed to King's strategy of direct, non-violent action. Nevertheless there was much truth in his claim.

How successful was the boycott? Montgomery buses were desegregated and blacks had shown what non-violent protests could achieve. However, King's prominence upset many. A friend noted that,

King's colleagues felt that he was taking too many bows and enjoying them ... he was forgetting that victory ... had been the result of collective thought and collective action.[12]

There were also disagreements as to the best way forward. NAACP favoured litigation; King preferred mass action. Both strategies were important, for it was a November 1957 Supreme Court ruling, inspired by the mass black action, that finally ended segregation on Montgomery buses. However, soon after, litigation failed in Birmingham, Alabama, and a bus boycott failed in Rock Hill, South Carolina.

SCLC (see page 70) grew out of the Montgomery experiences. Early SCLC rallies were effectively sabotaged by NAACP which considered SCLC a superfluous rival. Was it wise of King to set up a new organisation? NAACP was a national organisation. Southerners dominated SCLC, which concentrated on the South, an area that had very specific problems that needed addressing. Furthermore, Southern NAACP members suffered great persecution after BROWN. It was far harder for Southern racists to attack a church-dominated organisation such as SCLC. SCLC wanted to offer an alternative to NAACP's litigation strategy, that is, direct non-violent action. CORE had tried that, mostly in the North, but CORE currently lacked dynamism. The National Urban League concentrated on improving life in the Northern cities. Perhaps the time was ripe for a new organisation. Studying SCLC's achievements enables us to decide whether the new organisation was necessary.

b) SCLC (1957–60)

When King was elected president of SCLC (January 1957) he acquired responsibility for masterminding a civil rights campaign in the South. A main element of his strategy was to attract national attention to racial inequality. He began with one of his favourite tactics, a march, the high point of which would be his eloquent exposition of black problems. He masterminded a pilgrimage to Washington. He was the most popular speaker before a crowd of around 20,000 outside the Lincoln Memorial (May 1957).

One-off events such as marches were relatively easy to organise and gained maximum publicity for minimum work. Sustained local campaigns for specific gains proved more difficult for SCLC. Poor organisation and the lack of salaried staff and of mass support hampered SCLC's 'Crusade for Citizenship', which aimed to encourage Southern blacks to vote.

In 1959, King admitted that SCLC had achieved little in its first thirty-six months. He therefore gave up his Montgomery ministry and moved to Atlanta to concentrate on SCLC. As always, one of the greatest organisational problems he faced was local and national black divisions. Atlanta's black leaders were unenthusiastic about SCLC. 'Jealousy among [national] black leaders is so thick it can be cut with a knife', said the *Pittsburgh Courier*. For example, King wanted to gain publicity for the cause by picketing the Democratic and Republican conventions. Adam Clayton Powell opposed the idea and said that if King did that, he would 'go public' with the accusation that King had a physical relationship with an associate who had been prosecuted for homosexual activity with two other men in a parked car. The picketing in Los Angeles and Chicago went ahead, but failed to attract much support or attention.

Most historians consider organisation one of King's great weaknesses. SCLC's early disorganisation and lack of inspiration seem to prove that.

c) SNCC and Sit-ins (1960)

King admitted that SCLC achieved little in the three years after Montgomery. Then the civil rights movement exploded into life again (February 1960). Initially, King had nothing to do with it.

It began in Greensboro, North Carolina. Four black college students spontaneously refused to leave the all-white Woolworth's cafeteria when asked. Other students took up and retained the seats, day after day, forcing the cafeteria to close. Ominously for black unity, the NAACP was unenthusiastic about helping the students and disgruntled SCLC employee Ella Baker warned them not to let adults like King take over their protest. The 'sit-ins' spread across the South. These students were better educated than their parents and more impatient with the slow progress toward equality. Responsibility for this mass action can be attributed to the original four, or the students who joined them, or the other black protesters who had pioneered the same technique in Oklahoma and Kansas in 1957–8, or the press. The press had ignored the 1957–8 actions yet covered Greensboro.

Whites pour food on a black and white student 'sit-in' at the Woolworth's lunch counter, Jackson, Mississippi, May 1963.

King's talk of non-violent protest might have been inspirational. King had his own ideas as to who was responsible for the movement. A Greensboro SCLC member contacted King who quickly arrived to encourage the students and assure them of full SCLC support, saying, 'What is new in your fight is the fact that it was initiated, fed, and sustained by students.' Atlanta students begged King to join them in sit-ins. As in Montgomery, King was led rather than leading.

The sit-ins brought about some successes. Atlanta's schools and stores were soon desegregated. Black students had been mobilised, although when they set up the Student Non-Violent Co-ordinating Committee (SNCC) inter-organisational strife arose. SNCC/SCLC relations were soon as bad as NAACP/SCLC relations. SNCC accused SCLC of keeping donations intended for SNCC. When King publicly acknowledged NAACP/SCLC divisions, Roy Wilkins was furious. Blacks desperately needed a single leader who could unite all activists. King never managed to fulfil that role, but others such as the prickly Wilkins were probably far more culpable than he.

d) The Freedom Rides (1961)

Although King seemed unable to think up new tactics for gaining attention, CORE's 'Freedom Ride' (May 1961) electrified the civil rights movement. A small integrated group travelled the South testing Supreme Court rulings against segregation on interstate transport (1946) and on interstate bus facilities (1960). The tactic had been used before (1947) to no great effect. Now CORE's director James Farmer explained that,

1   We planned the Freedom Ride with the specific intention of creating a
     crisis. We were counting on the bigots in the South to do our work for
     us. We figured that the government would have to respond if we cre-
     ated a situation that was headline news all over the world, and affected
5   the nation's image abroad.[13]

As expected, Alabama racists attacked black passengers with clubs and chains and burned their buses. King quickly made contact with the riders. Students criticised King for not going on the rides himself, but as he was on probation for a minor traffic offence he feared arrest.

Although CORE initiated the Freedom Rides, King used them to get CORE, SCLC, and SNCC to work together – or to ensure SCLC domination, his critics said. All agreed that the aim was publicity. It worked. Attorney General Bobby Kennedy effectively ended segregation in interstate travel in November 1961. However, black divisions remained. CORE insisted SCLC announce that CORE had originated the Freedom Ride!

King's first 18 months in Atlanta had been productive. Despite tensions, SCLC, CORE, NAACP, the National Urban League, and the SNCC all agreed to work together on voter registration. SCLC was better organised, better financed, and more united. It was agreed that some members could concentrate on protests, others on voter registration. The students had resolved the debate about the relative merits of litigation or direct action in favour of the latter. The Freedom Rides had forced the government into action. King was learning how to use the media. The sit-ins, the Freedom Rides and King's imprisonment had all helped to confirm his leadership of America's blacks. One of the characteristics of his leadership was that he did not mind being led by others, so long as the tactics were working.

e) Albany (1961–2)

In November 1961 others led the way again. SNCC mobilised students from (black) Albany State College, Georgia to protest against segregation and disfranchisement. Local NAACP representatives were hostile and some local blacks regarded SNCC as troublemakers. The students challenged segregation in Albany bus station. Hundreds of freedom riders were arrested. The city authorities refused to desegregate, despite a Supreme Court ruling against segregated interstate transport terminals and pressure from Attorney General Kennedy.

Once again King was led rather than leading. Older leaders of the

'Albany Movement' invited him to join them. This angered SNCC leaders who stressed that the Albany Movement was 'by and for local Negroes'. King told a reporter, 'The people wanted to do something they would have done with or without me.'

King led a march and got himself arrested. Movement leaders and the city authorities agreed that demonstrators would be released from prison, protests would stop, and a biracial committee would be set up. However, after King left, the authorities reneged on the agreement. The Albany Movement petered out in a series of decreasingly supported protests. King recognised Albany as his first major defeat. The interstate terminal facilities were desegregated, and more black voters were allowed to register, but the city closed the parks, sold the swimming pool, integrated the library only after removing all the seats, and refused to desegregate the schools.

Why had the Albany Movement failed? While blacks got bad publicity for some violence, the local police chief had carefully avoided violence, so the federal government had not had to intervene. 'The key to everything is federal commitment,' said King. Black divisions were crucial: some were paid informants of the white city leadership. Local black leaders resented 'outsiders'. NAACP, SNCC and SCLC failed to co-operate. Some of King's associates thought him indecisive over these black squabbles. Blacks criticised him for choosing a fine rather than remaining in Albany jail for Christmas as he had promised.

Had anything been achieved? Local black leaders claimed the black community had lost a lot of its fear of white power. The entire black community had been mobilised. National attention had been gained. King learned it was unwise for SCLC to intervene in an area without a strong SCLC presence and that it was probably more effective to focus upon one particular aspect of segregation. King said that as blacks had little political power, it was unwise to concentrate upon negotiations with the white authorities; it made more sense to boycott white businesses so businessmen would advocate negotiations. All these lessons showed the best way forward in Birmingham, Alabama.

f) Birmingham (1963)

In 1963, King concentrated upon segregation and unequal opportunities in Birmingham, Alabama. Why Birmingham? Faced with competing civil rights organisations, SCLC had to demonstrate it could be dynamic and successful. SNCC and NAACP were relatively inactive in Birmingham, where the local black leader was affiliated to SCLC and King's own brother was a pastor. While King expected fewer crippling black divisions, white divisions looked promising. While white businessmen felt racism held the city back, white extremists had recently castrated a Negro, prohibited sale of a book that featured black and white rabbits, and campaigned to stop 'Negro music' being played on white radio stations. Birmingham could be expected to produce the kind of violent white opposition that won national sympathy. King described Birmingham as 'by far' America's 'worst big city' for racism. Unlike Albany's self-controlled police chief, Birmingham's Public Safety Commissioner 'Bull' Connor was a hot tempered and determined segregationist who had dared to clash with Eleanor Roosevelt years before. Connor had ensured that Freedom Riders under attack from a racist Birmingham mob had not received protection from his police, whom he gave the day off because it was Mother's Day! Bull and Birmingham would show the media segregation at its worst. Finally, King was impatient with the Kennedy administration's inactivity. The Freedom Riders had shown that violence forced federal intervention. 'To cure injustices,' said King, 'you must expose them before the light of human conscience and the bar of public opinion.'

Unlike Albany, SCLC's Birmingham actions were carefully planned. King was leading rather than being led. However, he made miscalculations. SCLC failed to recruit enough local demonstrators, because the local SCLC leader was unpopular. Many blacks felt the recent electoral defeat and imminent retirement of Connor made action unnecessary. King admitted there was 'tremendous resistance' amongst blacks to his planned demonstrations. SCLC had to use demonstrators in areas where there were lots of blacks to give the impression of mass action and to encourage onlookers to participate.

Then, as expected, Connor attracted national attention. His police and their dogs turned on black demonstrators. King defied an injunction and marched, knowing his arrest would gain national attention and perhaps inspire others. He was kept in solitary confinement and not allowed private meetings with his lawyer. He wrote an inspirational 'Letter from Birmingham Jail', partly on prison toilet paper. Coretta called President Kennedy, who got King released.

It remained difficult to mobilise sufficient demonstrators. Despite considerable local opposition, SCLC enlisted black school children. 'You know,' said King, 'we've got to get something going. The press is leaving.' Although King doubted the morality of using the children (some aged only six) it was very successful. 500 young marchers were soon in custody. Birmingham was headlines again. Connor's high-pressure water hoses tore clothes off students' backs. Blacks threw rocks and bottles at his police dogs. 'I want to see the dogs work. Look at those niggers run,' a reporter heard Connor say. SCLC succeeded in its aim of 'filling the jails'. A leading SCLC official 'praised' Bull Connor:

1   Birmingham would have been lost if Bull had let us go down to the City Hall and pray; if he had let us do that and stepped aside, what else would be new? There would be no movement, no publicity. But all he could see was stopping us before we got there. We had calculated for
5   the stupidity of a Bull Connor. He was a perfect adversary. Connor wanted publicity, he wanted his name in the paper. He believed that he would be the state's most popular politician if he treated the black violently, bloodily, and sternly.[14]

Birmingham was now in chaos. Whites and blacks were using violence. The school authorities were concerned about the truancy of student protesters. President Kennedy concluded that the turmoil was 'damaging the reputation' of Birmingham and America. King therefore called for a one-day halt to the demonstrations, but that infuriated the local black leader:

1   Well, Martin, you know they said in Albany that you come in, get people
     excited and started, and you leave town ... Oh, you've got a press con-
     ference? I thought we were to make joint statements. Now Martin,
     you're mister big but you're soon-to-be mister nothing.... You're
5   mister big, but you're going to be mister S-H-I-T.[15]

A deal was reached to desegregate stores, improve black job opportunities, and have biracial talks, but white extremists tried to sabotage the agreement. Connor's Ku Klux Klan friends got involved. Bombs hit King's brother's house and King's motel room. State troopers (commanded by a friend of both Connor and of Alabama's racist Governor George Wallace) disappeared from guarding the motel just before the explosion. Blacks began to riot. A policeman was stabbed. Bobby Kennedy feared this could trigger off nationwide violence, and urged his brother to protect the Birmingham agreement. Bobby told reporters that King was relatively moderate: 'If King loses, worse leaders are going to take his place.' When conservatives in the

A black demonstrator attacked by Bull Connor's police dogs, Birmingham, Alabama, 1963. An SCLC worker said the demonstrator was trying to stop other blacks responding to police violence.

Birmingham educational establishment tried to de-rail the settlement by expelling 1100 students for having skipped classes to demonstrate, King persuaded local black leaders not to call for a total boycott of all schools and businesses, but to take the cases to court. They did so, and a federal judge got the students reinstated.

Birmingham was the first time that King had really led the movement. Had he got it right? There had been miscalculations. Only the high school students had given SCLC the necessary numerical support. However, rioting black teenagers had helped convince the business community to desegregate. SCLC's accidental discovery of how black bystanders could contribute to the cause had also been a tactical breakthrough. SCLC had correctly assessed how Connor would react and how the media would depict his reactions. 'There never was any more skilful manipulation of the news media than there was in Birmingham,' said a leading SCLC staffer. SCLC had shown America that Southern segregation was very unpleasant, which was far more important than the speed of desegregation in Birmingham stores. Extra donations poured into SCLC. The Kennedy administration admitted that Birmingham was crucial in persuading them to introduce civil rights legislation. 'We are on the threshold of a significant breakthrough,' said King, 'and the greatest weapon is the mass demonstration.' In the summer of 1963 protests throughout the South owed inspiration to Birmingham. King had shown that he could lead from the front and gain change, but through rather artificially engineered violence which could lose him both popularity and credibility, were it to get out of hand.

g) The March on Washington (1963)

Marches were a favourite tactic of civil rights activists, and Washington DC a favourite location. The Washington March of August 1963 revealed the problems and opportunities of inter-organisational co-operation. It aimed to encourage passage of a civil rights bill and executive action to help blacks. It would obviously be far more effective if all the black organisations participated, but Roy Wilkins was not supportive. Nor was President Kennedy. Their opposition worried King. King felt the march would maintain black morale and advertise the effectiveness of non-violent protest. He feared non-violence was losing popularity. 'The Negro is shedding himself of his fear,' he said, 'and my real worry is how we will keep this fearlessness from rising to violent proportions.' He knew the slow pace of change embittered many blacks. He recognised that many Southern blacks used non-violence 'as a strategy', but had no real Christian love for whites. He knew violence brought change but he worried about the morality of it. He recognised that non-violent demonstrations 'make people inflict violence on you, so you precipitate violence.' However, he excused it: 'We are merely bringing to the surface the tension that has always been at the heart of the problem'.[16]

Wilkins finally agreed to participate, and the Washington March was a great success. The crowd was around a quarter of a million. A quarter of them were white. King's memorable speech emotionally appealed to documents and beliefs enshrined by white American history, for example, the Declaration of Independence, with its 'all men are created equal'. Naturally, his speeches were virtual sermons, with appeals to the Bible, and the typically black emphasis on the Old Testament God who freed his enslaved people. That appealed to America's Christians and Jews of all colours. In short, he uniquely and repeatedly tapped the emotional well springs of American history and culture, in such a way as to lead thoughtfully patriotic whites to conclude that King's dreams of equality should be made a reality:

1 I say to you today, my friends, so even though we face the difficulties of today and tomorrow, I still have a dream. It is a dream deeply rooted in the American dream. I have a dream that one-day this nation will rise up and live out the true meaning of its creed – we hold these truths to
5 be self-evident, that all men are created equal.
    I have a dream that one-day on the red hills of Georgia, the sons of former slaves and the sons of former slave owners will be able to sit down together at the table of brotherhood ...
    I have a dream that my four little children will one-day live in a nation
10 where they will not be judged by the colour of their skin but by the content of their character. I have a dream today!
    I have a dream that one-day, down in Alabama, with its vicious racists ... little black boys and black girls will be able to join hands with little white boys and white girls as sisters and brothers. I have a dream today! ...
15 Let freedom ring.... When we allow freedom to ring, when we let it ring from every village and every hamlet, from every state and every city, we will be able to speed up that day when all of God's children – black men and white men, Jews and Gentiles, Protestants and Catholics – will be able to join hands and sing in the words of the old Negro spiri-
20 tual, 'Free at last, free at last; thank God Almighty, we are free at last.'[17]

This was King the leader at his best, involved in an action the morality of which could not be doubted, and the quality of which he raised immeasurably by helping to persuade Wilkins to participate and by making a superb speech. Historians disagree over the extent to which the March was significant. Some say its emotional impact probably helped the passage of civil rights legislation.[18] Many contemporaries were thrilled by the speech, apart from Coretta, who was annoyed that she had not been invited to accompany her husband to see Kennedy!

h) What To Do Next

King was often accused of indecisive leadership. One of the best illustrations of his indecision was in winter 1963–4. There were great tensions and debates at SCLC over whether to concentrate on the Citizenship Education Programme or upon direct action, which was more glamorous and emotionally satisfying. King preferred theatrical demonstrations to voter registration campaigns. When CORE threatened to cut off access to the Brooklyn World Fair many moderate whites were alienated. Conservative black opposition disappointed King:

1 Indeed, we are engaged in the social revolution.... It is a movement to bring about certain basic structural changes in the architecture of American society. This is certainly revolutionary. My only hope is that it will remain a non-violent revolution ... we do not need allies who are
5 more devoted to ORDER than to JUSTICE ...[19]

King was unsure what to do next. SCLC believed that a limited focus on one city gave a greater chance for success. But which city? And what to do there? Three alternatives were considered. King announced his increasing concern over the ghettos of the North. However, when New York City's mayor asked King to help stop the black rioting triggered by a white policeman shooting a black youth, King's visit proved unproductive. The mayor was uncompromising, while some Harlem blacks called King an 'Uncle Tom'.

Another alternative was Birmingham, where little had changed. A bomb killed four young black girls attending Sunday School. The three whites arrested were freed for lack of evidence. Blacks rioted on the streets, and pelted police with rocks and rubbish. Policemen fired over the heads of the crowd and shot a black youth. King felt it vital to 'emerge with a clear-cut victory' in Birmingham, 'the symbol, the beginning of the revolution' where SCLC's reputation was at stake. However, Birmingham's black leaders said they did not want 'outside help' or 'outside interference'.

The third alternative was St Augustine, Florida, where there was considerable violence. King received Ku Klux Klan death threats, and said SCLC had never worked in a city 'as lawless as this'. St Augustine's white leadership refused to negotiate. An integrated group of seven protesters tried a new tactic – a 'swim-in' in a motel pool. The motel owner poured gallons of pool cleaning chemicals into the pool in vain. A policeman had to drag them out. Klansmen attacked police who tried to protect marchers. When the Klan picketed and fire-bombed places that had reluctantly desegregated, most of St Augustine re-segregated. King was keen to get out of the St Augustine impasse. SCLC had failed to get much support from local black leaders, but those who had supported King were embittered by his departure. On the other hand, some historians believe that although President Johnson refused to send in federal forces, the violent scenes of St Augustine helped get the civil rights bill through.[20]

King had thus temporarily reverted to a reactive rather than a proactive policy. There is no doubt that the cumulative effect of all the demonstrations and protests in which he played such a large part had been to help ensure the passage of the Civil Rights Act (July 1964). However, there was always a danger that nothing would change in practice. SNCC, CORE and SCLC activists had tried but failed to register a significant proportion of black voters but only two million out of the possible five million Southern black voters were registered. In Mississippi only 6.4% were registered. It was time to force the issue. Despite the Civil Rights Act, little had changed in Selma, Alabama. Blacks constituted the majority of Selma's 29,000 population, but only 3% of its electorate.

i) Selma (1965)

LIFE IN SELMA BEFORE 1965

Pre-Civil War Selma was surrounded by cotton plantations, each with a columned white mansion, encircled by magnolias dripping with Spanish moss. Black slaves worked in the cotton fields. Even after the abolition of slavery, racial divisions remained rigid. In 1960, about half of Selma's 29,000 population was black. Blacks had segregated schools, buses, churches, restaurants, playgrounds, public toilets and drinking fountains. They used a different library and swimming pool. They could only have certain jobs and houses. In white neighbourhoods the streets were paved. In black neighbourhoods there were dirt roads. The average white family income was four times that of black families. The local newspapers kept the black and white news separate. Despite an SNCC campaign, only 23 blacks were registered to vote. Lawsuits initiated by Robert Kennedy's Justice Department were still bogged down in the courts. The Civil Rights Act of 1964 had not brought any great improvements.

Concentration on Selma was the most specific thing SCLC had done for a year, a year in which King said he and the others had 'failed to assert the leadership the movement needed'. Why Selma? King announced Selma 'has become a symbol of bitter-end resistance to the civil rights movement in the Deep South'. It promised exploitable divisions within the white community. While some local black activists feared SCLC would 'come into town and leave too soon' or ignore them, others said that as SNCC had lost its dynamism there it was an ideal opportunity for SCLC. Selma's white officials could be trusted to react as brutally as Bull Connor, which would result in nationwide publicity and revitalise SCLC and the whole civil rights movement.

King led would-be voters to register at Selma County Court house. However, despite a federal judge's ruling, there were no registrations. Several incidents made headlines. A trooper shot a black youth who was trying to shield his mother from a club. Whites threw venomous snakes at blacks trying to register. King publicly admitted that he wanted to be arrested to publicise the fact that Selma blacks were not allowed to register to vote. A brilliant King letter was published in the *New York Times*:

> THIS IS SELMA, ALABAMA. THERE ARE MORE NEGROES IN JAIL WITH ME THAN THERE ARE ON THE VOTING ROLLS.

However, Selma had not proved as explosive as King had hoped. SCLC and SNCC therefore organised a march from Selma to Montgomery (Alabama's capital) to publicise the need for a Voting Rights Act. 80 Alabama whites joined the march. State troopers attacked the marchers with clubs and used tear gas. 'Bloody Sunday' aroused nationwide criticism of Selma's whites.

President Johnson asked King to call off the next march, but King felt that constituted a betrayal of his followers. Without informing SNCC, King got the marchers to approach the state troopers then retreat. SNCC felt betrayed and accused him of cowardice.

WERE ALL SOUTHERN WHITES 'BAD'?

Bob Zellner was the son of an Alabama Methodist minister. Looking back on the segregated society of his youth, he recalled: 'It was just the way things were. You didn't think about it. Sometimes when you are inside the system, you can't see it very well.' At college, he became sympathetic to the civil rights movement. The Ku Klux Klan threatened him. He joined SNCC and got jailed for working on voter registration in Mississippi. He joined a Mississippi march in protest against the murder of a black SNCC worker. He marched from Selma to Montgomery. His grandfather and uncle were Ku Klux Klan members and they threatened to kill him if he persisted. As blacks grew more suspicious of white assistance, he was excluded from SNCC. From 1967 he helped underpaid black and white workers.

How significant was Selma? The historian Stephen Oates described it as 'the movement's finest hour'.[21] King thought the nationwide criticism of 'Bloody Sunday' in Selma was 'a shining moment in the conscience of man'. There were sympathetic interracial marches in cities such as Chicago, Detroit, New York and Boston. Johnson and Congress probably would not have delivered the Voting Rights Act (August 1965) without Selma. On the other hand, although NAACP had been very supportive in the law courts, there were black divisions. SNCC publicly criticised SCLC: all SCLC ever left behind was 'a string of embittered cities' such as St Augustine, which were worse off than when SCLC had first got there; SCLC just used people in those cities to make a point. Disgruntled St Augustine black activists claimed King and SCLC had 'screwed' them. One said, 'I don't want him back here now.' Selma's activists felt betrayed by SCLC's withdrawal. SCLC had raised a great deal of money because Selma was in the headlines, then SCLC left and spent the money elsewhere. SNCC gleefully quoted an arrogant SCLC representative who said, 'They need us more than we need them. We can bring the press in with us and they can't.' SNCC also accused SCLC of 'leader worship' of King. However, black divisions were about to become even worse.

j) The Meredith March (1966)

A chance occurrence triggered off the first major non-violent protest since Selma fifteen months before. James Meredith, famous as the University of Mississippi's first black student (1962), planned a 220-mile walk from Memphis to Mississippi's capital Jackson, to encourage blacks to vote. He was shot on the second day of his walk and temporarily immobilised. Black organisations therefore declared that they would continue his walk. King and 20 others began the walk. There were 400 marchers by the third day, including the new SNCC leader, Stokely Carmichael. Born in the West Indies, brought up in Harlem, and educated at Howard, Carmichael was a founder member of SNCC. Charismatic, handsome and a good organiser, he was involved in SNCC's voter registration campaigns in Mississippi.

Black divisions damaged the march. NAACP and the National Urban League wanted the march to focus national attention on the new civil rights bill, and withdrew when Carmichael criticised the bill. King welcomed white participants, SNCC rejected them. SNCC and CORE had become increasingly militant, following the lack of federal protection for their voter registration projects in the 'Mississippi Freedom Summer' of 1964. Carmichael was arrested. Upon release, he urged the burning of 'every courthouse in Mississippi' and demanded 'black power'. Crowds took up the chant. As white bystanders waved Confederate flags, shouted obscenities and threw things at the marchers, SNCC people sang:

> Jingle bells, shotgun shells, Freedom all the way,
> Oh what fun it is to blast, A [white] trooper man away.

King and SCLC tried to encourage chants of 'freedom now'. King disliked 'black power', because the words would alienate white sympathisers and encourage a white backlash. Tired of violence, King urged blacks to avoid violent retaliation against tear gas. He begged Johnson to send in federal troops but, as in Selma, Johnson refused.

Meanwhile Meredith felt excluded and began a march of his own! Some SCLC leaders joined him to disguise the split. The 15,000 main marchers ended at Jackson with rival chants of 'black power' and 'freedom now'. King despaired. 'I don't know what I'm going to do.

The government has got to give me some victories if I'm going to keep people non-violent.' He felt he could no longer co-operate with SNCC. 'Because Stokely Carmichael chose the March as an arena for a debate over black power,' King told the press, 'we did not get to emphasise the evils of Mississippi and the need for the 1966 Civil Rights Act.' He admitted that blacks were 'very, very close' to a public split. NAACP no longer wanted to co-operate with SCLC or SNCC.

King had frequently been led by others, but had previously managed to put himself at the forefront of their movements. Now it seemed likely that leadership might pass into the hands of extremists such as Carmichael who rejected 'passive resistance'.

k) Watts (1965)

On Friday 13th August 1965, riots erupted in Los Angeles' Watts ghetto. Black mobs set fire to several blocks of stores. Local churchmen asked King for help. Despite his previously unsuccessful intervention in New York, King felt it was his duty. The scenes of devastation in Watts shocked him. Bayard Rustin, King's ex-Communist friend, recalled how King was

> absolutely undone, and he looked at me and said, 'You know, Bayard, I worked to get these people the right to eat hamburgers, and now I've got to do something ... to help them get the money to buy it' ... I think it was the first time he really understood.[22]

King told the press this had been 'a class revolt of underprivileged against privileged ... the main issue is economic'. Others were leading the leader toward a new philosophy. Previously King had thought of 'freedom' in the traditional American sense of the democratic right to vote. That right had been confirmed for blacks by the recent legislation but other grievances remained in the poverty stricken ghettos. Now King began to define 'freedom' in terms of economic equality rather than political equality. He was turning to socialism, calling for 'a better distribution of the wealth' of America.

l) Going North

Southern blacks had sought and gained primarily political rights. Now King turned North. There the problem was economic and social rights. King had thought the struggle in the South would help Northern blacks. It had not. He had to do something to stop the increasing tendency toward violence and radicalism amongst blacks. King therefore sought a Northern city upon which SCLC could concentrate. He chose Chicago. Why? SCLC said: 'if Northern problems can be solved there, they can be solved anywhere.' Chicago was America's second-largest city, with a three million population, 700,000 of whom were black. Chicago blacks suffered chronic employment, housing and education problems. In October 1963 over half of Chicago's black students boycotted their inferior, segregated schools for a day in protest but no improvement had resulted. Other great Northern cities were effectively shut off to King. Powell told him to keep out of New York City. A Philadelphia NAACP leader behaved similarly. Although Chicago activists warned SCLC not to just 'come in and take over', they did so relatively amicably. Chicago's influential religious community supported the civil rights movement. King hoped he could demonstrate his leadership skills for the first time in the North, which he thought suffered from 'bankruptcy of leadership'. Chicago's Mayor Daley had a unique political domination; if he could be won over, things could get done. Chicago could become an inspirational symbol.

However, there were problems. King and his lieutenant, Andrew Young, did not know what SCLC could do in Chicago: 'we do not have a programme yet for the North'. Young talked vaguely of mobilising Chicago blacks, and 'pulling things together'. King knew that Northern opponents would be more 'subtle' than Southerners like Bull Connor. Some Chicago blacks felt non-violence was ineffectual, while others were Daley clients. NAACP was unhelpful.

SCLC rented a Chicago ghetto apartment for King's use during the campaign. Once the landlord found out who his new tenant was, an army of repair men moved in to make it habitable. The Chicago press and ghetto dwellers watched with amusement, and joked that the easiest way for King to improve ghetto housing would be for him to move from building to building! King led reporters around rat infested, unheated ghetto dwellings. King and his aides dramatically seized a Chicago slum building and, dressed in work clothes, began repairing it. King told the press that SCLC had collected the tenants' rents to finance this. When he said that moral questions were more important than legal ones in this case, the press cried 'ANARCHY!' The usual divisions between local Chicago activists and SCLC members materialised and the lack of a clearly defined issue did not help. The July 1966 Chicago rally turnout was 30,000, disappointingly below the anticipated 100,000. The subsequent meeting between King and Daley was unproductive. King said Daley did too little, Daley said he did his best.

King's own family neared disintegration as they sampled Chicago ghetto life. There were neither pools nor parks in which his children could escape the suffocating heat of their small, airless flat. The surrounding streets were too crowded and dangerous to play in. King's children screamed and fought each other, as never before. A few days later, with the temperature near 100 degrees, the police shut off a fire hydrant that black youths had been using to cool themselves. After some youths were arrested, angry blacks ran through the streets. King persuaded the police to release the youngsters. King encouraged ministers to join him in walking the ghetto streets to try to calm people.

Black crowds derided and walked away from him, but he persuaded Mayor Daley to make fire hydrants and pools available.

Chicago whites feared black neighbours would hit property values, increase crime, and threaten cultural homogeneity. So, when 500 black marchers defiantly and provocatively entered a white Chicago neighbourhood to publicise the fact that they could not as yet reside there, they were greeted with rocks, bottles, and cries of 'apes', 'cannibals', 'savages', and 'The only way to stop niggers is to exterminate them'. Several such incidents occurred. The police, shocked at being called 'nigger lovers' by fellow whites, did little to protect the blacks. When a rock hit King, it made the national press. The marches then became more peaceful: 800 policeman protected seven hundred marchers on one occasion. Many influential whites blamed King for the riots and invited him to leave. King himself blamed Daley. 'A nonviolent movement cannot maintain its following unless it brings about change.' He warned that discriminatory house-selling practices would lead to 'Negro cities ringed with white suburbs', which was dangerous: hatred and fear developed when people were thus separated. The *Chicago Tribune* denounced King as a 'paid professional agitator' and asked how he could justify demonstrations that turned violent. He said demonstrations might stop greater violence.

1   and let me say that if you are tired of demonstrations, I am tired of demonstrating . . . for something that should have been mine at first. . . . We are not trying to overthrow you; we are trying to get in . . . your second point about the demonstrations being the wrong approach bothers me,
5   because the problem is not created by the marches. A doctor doesn't cause cancer when he finds it . . . you know we don't have much. We don't have much money [nor] education, and we don't have political power . . . you are asking us to give up the one thing that we have when you say, 'Don't march'. . . . We are being asked to stop one of our most
10   precious rights, the right to assemble, the right to petition. . . . We're trying to keep the issue so alive that it will be acted on. Our marching feet have brought us a long way, and if we hadn't marched I don't think we'd be here today . . .[23]

In autumn 1966 King left Chicago, leaving SCLC's dynamic young Jesse Jackson in charge of 'Operation Breadbasket' which successfully used economic boycotts to help increase black employment.

In Chicago, King had tried to lead. What had he achieved? Because of the threat of black marches into racist white areas, Daley agreed to promote integrated housing in Chicago, but the agreement was a mere 'paper victory' (*Chicago Daily News*). Most blacks remained stranded in the ghetto. Although SCLC obtained a $4 million federal grant to improve Chicago housing and left behind a significant legacy of community action, local blacks felt SCLC had 'sold out' and lapsed into apathy. An SCLC staffer in Chicago said the voter registration drive there was' a nightmare', 'largely because of division in the

Negro leadership' and partly because Chicago blacks were disinterested. 'I have never seen such hopelessness.' 'A lot of people won't even talk to us.' Chicago's race relations had always been poor (see page 37). King could be considered to have worsened the situation. Black hopes were raised then dashed, and there was a white backlash. Whites increasingly thought of blacks as troublemakers on welfare.

The *New Republic* said, 'so far, King has been pretty much of a failure at organising.' One of King's closest admirers described the Chicago venture as a 'fiasco' and 'disaster'. Why had it failed? The anti-Vietnam war movement was taking funds and energies from the civil rights movement. SCLC had been inadequately briefed and ill-prepared – they even lacked warm clothing for the Chicago winter. There were the usual black divisions. The local black churches had not co-operated with each other. They lacked the prestige and organisational skills of Southern churches. Mayor Daley was unhelpful. He did not want to alienate his white working class voters. He detested King, calling him a 'dirty sonofabitch, a bastard, a prick ... a rabble-rouser, a trouble-maker'. The problem with the Chicago tactics was that an agreement arrived at through fear and intimidation was hard to maintain once the fear had passed. This was not the answer for the North. King was unrealistic in thinking that SCLC could effect a social and economic revolution in Chicago within months. He and Ella Baker had always disagreed about the relative merits of demonstrations and grass-roots organisation down South, where SCLC's failure to develop grass-roots participation often lead to disaster, as in St Augustine. SCLC had always favoured autocratic organisation, driven by top-down participation. King would go into a St Augustine and hope to effect a miraculous transformation without necessarily educating and organising the local population for a long-term haul after he and the media had gone. The top-down style had nevertheless had many successes down South, as with Birmingham and Selma. However, these tactical weaknesses proved King's undoing in Chicago, where King and SCLC had failed to educate and organise the local population. While Jesse Jackson thought Chicago was a success, because it had woken up Northern black America, that awakening led to violence in the Northern ghettos. Coretta King considered that violence was counter-productive: it 'unleashed' the 'vastly superior' white force that her husband had predicted.

m) 'Where Do We Go From Here?'

After the Chicago debacle, King was depressed and unsure what to do next. He was marginalised by black extremists such as Carmichael, who called for black and white separation, and said blacks should use 'any means necessary' to obtain their rights. Black extremists, the white backlash and the distraction of white liberals by the Vietnam War resulted in the collapse of the civil rights coalition that had effected so much. In his book *Where Do We Go From Here?* (1967), King highlighted the problem: political concessions to blacks had not cost money. The economic improvement that blacks now sought would cost whites money. No one likes paying taxes. King tried to point the way forward: blacks should not to be discouraged when whites pointed out that other immigrants had prospered – they had not suffered enslavement. He urged black pride in the past, and hard work for the future. He urged demonstrations to seek affirmative action, on the grounds that 'a society that has done something against the Negro for hundreds of years must now do something special for him, in order to equip him to compete on a just and equal basis'.[24] Finally, King urged blacks to broaden their movement and bring the Hispanic, Indian and white Appalachian poor into the war on poverty. He planned to bring all the poor together in a civil disobedience campaign wherein they would camp out in Washington. King had gone way beyond being a black civil rights leader. He had lost his old constituency, but not gained a new one. Adam Clayton Powell christened him 'Martin Loser King'. Even sympathisers expected his Poor People's Campaign to fail, to end in violence and an even greater white backlash. His final strategy (to represent a wider constituency) and his final tactics (yet another protest) were, in the climate of the time, unwise and unrealistic. Even friends and colleagues opposed his Poor People's Campaign. 'It's just isn't working. People aren't responding,' he admitted.

Others, who recognised his publicity value, orchestrated King's last public appearances. In March 1968, King was asked to visit Memphis, Tennessee, to give support to black sanitation workers faced with discrimination from the city authorities. King joined a protest march, wherein a radical black power minority got violent and broke shop windows. King was exhausted, confused, frightened and in despair. 'Maybe we just have to admit that the day of violence is here, and may be we have to just give up'. Within hours, King was dead.

n) Assessment of King's Leadership

We have seen that King was frequently led by others rather than leading them, but the end result was often satisfactory to him. His actions and involvement always gained national attention and sometimes provided the vital impetus for some reform. Sometimes his tactics and strategy were neither successful nor admirable. On the other hand, the problems blacks faced were long-standing and enormous, and his patience was criticised by people such as Stokely Carmichael. King did too little to satisfy 'black power' advocates, and too much for many whites, suggesting that his way was truly the middle way. His organisational skills were limited, but his ability to inspire was peerless. He was a relatively moderate leader who made a massive contribution to the black cause, but in so doing inevitably roused white and black antagonism and extremism in a nation in which blacks had been too long oppressed.

4 Uncle Tom or Radical Revolutionary?

> **KEY ISSUES** Was King slavishly respectable toward whites?
> Or was he a political, social and economic radical?

Contemporaries who accused King of deferring to white authority figures were usually young 'black power' militants who rejected non-violence and patience. He in turn criticised them. He told the *New York
Times* 'black power' was dangerous, provocative and costing the civil
rights movement support. King was uneasy about the 'hate whitey'
and anti-Semitic speeches of Malcolm X, a leader of the radical black
Nation of Islam. While Black Muslims said only physical violence
could defeat American racism, King knew violence stood little chance
against the military strength of the American government. King was
moderate in comparison yet even he aroused hatred and a refusal to
make concessions amongst many whites. The rectitude of King's philosophy of working with whites was demonstrated when CORE and
SNCC precipitated their self-destruction by expelling whites during
1966–7.

MALCOLM X AND THE NATION OF ISLAM

-Profile-

Malcolm Little's West Indian mother
and Baptist preacher father were
driven from their Nebraska home in
1926 because of involvement in
Marcus Garvey's black nationalist
movement. Malcolm claimed his
father was thrown to his death under
a tramcar by a white mob, but no
proof exists. Later, Malcolm bitterly
recalled how, as a ghetto youth, he
burned his scalp as he straightened
his hair in order to look like the 'superior' white race. Malcolm
spent his youth in petty crime, robbery, drug abuse and pimping.
In prison a Black Muslim of the Nation of Islam converted him.
He replaced his 'slave name' Little with 'X'.

The Nation of Islam was established in Detroit in 1930, and
spread throughout Northern cities in the 1950s. From 1933, its
leader was Elijah Muhammad, a Garvey-ite who said he was
'Allah's Prophet'. He believed Allah made all people black. An
evil black chemist created whites. Infuriated, Allah punished his
chosen black people by enslavement by white devils. On
Judgement Day, whites would be destroyed. The Black Muslims

were anti-Semitic and sexist. Elijah Muhammad said females were 'given to evil and sin while men are noble and given to righteousness.' Malcolm X said the best position for a woman was 'horizontal'. Black Muslims advocated racial separatism or 'return' to Africa. They preferred to be called 'Afro-American', not 'Negro'. Their strict moral code prohibited extra marital sex, smoking, alcohol and drugs. They rejected political or military activity. Malcolm X became their most famous minister (New York City, 1954). His preaching encouraged black pride, and his popularity amongst ghetto blacks contributed greatly to the Nation's $3 million annual income in 1959. In 1964 Malcolm left the Nation because he wanted to participate in the civil rights struggle and to make political comments on his 'sick country'. Elijah Muhammad resented Malcolm's increasing influence, while Malcolm resented Elijah Mohammed's hypocrisy over extra-marital sex.

When Malcolm X visited Mecca (1964) he felt he had found the real Muslim religion. While still advocating black nationalism and violence if necessary, he now countenanced black and white co-operation against racism. He apologised for his verbal attacks on King. Malcolm X was murdered, probably by fellow Muslims. The Nation of Islam subsequently fragmented and went into relative decline. It continued the black nationalist tradition of separatism, as opposed to Booker T. Washington's accommoda-tionism and Martin Luther King's integrationism as the solution to American race relations problems.

BLACK PANTHERS

Two black college students, Huey Newton and Bobby Seale, founded the Black Panthers in Oakland, California, in 1966. They demanded full employment, decent housing, 'black' history in schools, the release of all black prisoners from jail, trial by black jury and exemption from military service. Members carried guns and were considered a threat to law and order, especially when they espoused Communism. Police and FBI imprisonment and harassment destroyed them in the early 1970s.

King was no Uncle Tom. He frequently criticised presidential policies. Some of his demonstrations were deliberately provocative. They invited white violence, making nonsense of his advocacy of non-violence. Like the founder of the Christian religion he espoused, King was a social and economic radical. Initially, within the Southern context, King was a political radical who sought the vote for the disfranchised. The Northern ghettos convinced him that 'something is wrong with the economic system of our nation ... something is wrong with capitalism.' King's tactics could be considered revolutionary, particularly with his Poor People's Campaign. He envisaged representatives of all America's poor living in a temporary 'Resurrection City' in Washington, until Congress acted. King wanted to cause 'massive dislocation ... without destroying life or property.' Bringing Washington to a halt would be 'a kind of last, desperate demand for the nation to respond to nonviolence'.

By the winter of 1967–8 the Johnson administration considered King a revolutionary who advocated 'criminal [not civil] disobedience'. A close associate feels there now

> is a definite effort on the part of America to change Martin Luther King, Jr., from what he really was all about – to make him the Uncle Tom of the century. In my mind, he was the militant of the century.[25]

In 1995 King's family had a bitter argument with the federal National Park Service who played down the radicalism of King's later career in information they handed out at Atlanta's King National Historic site.

5 King's Achievements

> **KEY ISSUES** How much progress had been made toward equality, 1956–68? How much had King contributed to that progress?

Much had been achieved. Black activism had probably played the most important part in producing the legislation (see chapter 6) by which Southern segregation had been shattered and a mass black electorate had gained a voice in the political process. American blacks had gained greater self-confidence. However, much remained to be done. The ghettos were still a national disgrace. Black poverty remained endemic, but a start had been made by Johnson's Great Society legislation (see chapter 6). Was it all King's doing? The federal government played an important role as did white extremists. President Kennedy joked that Bull Connor was a hero of the civil rights movement! Many of King's fellow blacks played a vital role – organisations such as NAACP, CORE and SNCC, local community organisations, along with thousands of usually unsung field workers who educated, protested and sometimes inspired. Black churches played an important part, although possibly King's prominence has led to their being given excessive credit. A study of Louisiana showed that most black ministers were poor organisers and unhelpfully authoritarian on the rare occasions they initiated protest.[26] On the other hand, Christianity was a vital part of Southern black culture and it would be foolish to deny its central role in inspiring individuals within each organisation. Ella Baker not surprisingly insists 'the movement made Martin rather than Martin making the movement'.[27] He was no great organiser and was often led rather than leading, but even then, his fellow blacks usually wanted him with them. His ability to inspire was unique.

How significant was his death? Some claim his death stirred the conscience of white America more than his life. Carmichael said white racism had killed the one black man who was trying to teach blacks to love whites. The best way to judge the significance of his death is perhaps to look at what followed: the national direct action phase of the civil rights movement died with him. The Poor People's Campaign fizzled out under his successor Ralph Abernathy. SCLC imploded like SNCC and CORE, without King to keep his egotistic lieutenants together. On the other hand, it is not certain that the civil rights movement would have progressed any further had King lived. We have seen that King failed in Chicago. Other black activists were becoming more impatient and their frequent extremism was important in generating a white backlash.

References

1 Quoted by Anthony Badger, University of London lecture, 22nd February 1999.
2 Badger lecture.
3 Quoted in David Garrow, *Bearing the Cross*, Jonathan Cape, 1993, p. 33.
4 Ibid. 423.
5 Ibid., p. 58.
6 Ibid., p. 580.
7 Ibid., p. 598.
8 Ibid., p. 550.
9 Ibid., p. 375.
10 Ibid., p. 56.
11 Robert Cook, *Sweet Land of Liberty?*, Longman, 1998, p. 39.
12 Garrow, p. 89.
13 Ibid., p. 156.
14 Ibid., p. 251.
15 Ibid., pp. 256–7.
16 Ibid., pp. 273–4.
17 Ibid., pp. 283–4.
18 W.T.M Riches, 'Civil Rights Movement', Macmillan, 1997, pp. 73–4.
19 Garrow, p. 32.
20 Stephen Oates, *Let the Trumpet Sound*, Cannongate Books, 1998, p. 301.
21 Ibid., p. 365.
22 Garrow, p. 439.
23 Ibid., pp. 512–5.
24 Oates, p. 426.
25 Garrow, p. 625.
26 Adam Fairclough, *Race and Democracy: the Civil Rights Struggle in Louisiana, 1915–72*, Georgia, 1995, pp. 71–2.
27 Garrow, p. 625.

Summary Diagram

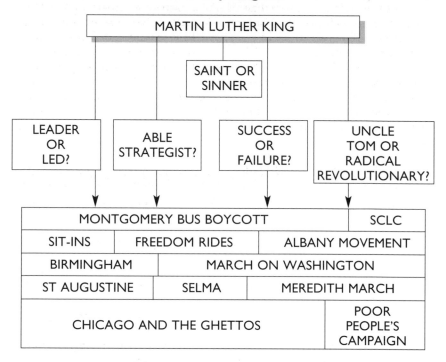

The important issue in this chapter is how much King contributed to the civil rights movement, 1956–68, and how much he achieved. There are 'fors and againsts' on both issues. Perhaps working in twos would be helpful. One could argue that others contributed more, and that little was achieved. The other could argue that King was the most important factor and that great progress was made. These debates can bring in arguments about his tactics – the advocate of 'others contributed more' will criticise his tactics, the opponent will defend them.

Answering structured and essay questions on Chapter 5

Think about this two-part question:

a) In what ways did blacks feel themselves discriminated against in the 1950s and 1960s? Account for that discrimination. (*15 marks*)
b) Was Malcolm X more significant than Martin Luther King in the civil rights movement? (*15 marks*)

The first question gives you a structure for your answer. It gives you a helpful reminder that your answer needs to be a mixture of pure factual recall (modes of discrimination) and analysis (reasons behind the discrimination). Now think about this question: 'Account for the opposition to Martin Luther King's attempts to improve the position of blacks in US society.' Take care when asked about opposition. Remember that 'the opposition' covers a very wide range of people. It includes those blacks and whites who hated him, some who were more neutral, and sometimes even those who loved him but opposed him on particular issues.

Answering source-based questions on Chapter 5

Look at the source extracts on pages 80–83, 85–86, 91–92, 94–95, 99, 101 and 106.

a) What is meant by (i) 'meaning of its creed' (page 94)? and (ii) 'the right to eat hamburgers' (page 99)? (*2 marks*)

b) Which would be more reliable for a historian assessing King's importance in the Montgomery Bus Boycott, King (page 85) or Wilkins (page 86)? (*5 marks*)

c) What are the advantages and disadvantages for the historian using the memoirs of King's friends and colleagues? (*6 marks*)

d) Looking at the sources and using your own knowledge, would you agree that King was 'the militant of the century'? (*12 marks*)

When asked to combine ideas from sources and your knowledge, try to deal with both simultaneously, rather than sources first, then knowledge. Take a point from a source, then confirm and/or disprove it from your own knowledge to help to ascertain the source's validity.

How Much did Presidents Kennedy and Johnson Contribute?

6

POINTS TO CONSIDER

You need to think about what improvements were made in American society after 1961, and who and what helped and hindered them. Weigh up the relative importance of Kennedy, Johnson, Congress, and ordinary people of all races. Keep referring back to chapter 5 to remind yourself of the contribution of Dr Martin Luther King Jr.

KEY DATES

1961	Freedom Rides began.
1962	University of Mississippi enrolment crisis. Non-discriminatory federal housing.
1963	Kennedy civil rights bill. Birmingham crisis. March on Washington.
1964	Johnson's War on Poverty. 24th Amendment. Civil Rights Act. Selma voter registration crisis.
1965	Voting Rights Act. Watts riots.
1966	Unsuccessful housing bill.
1967	King assassinated. Civil Rights Act.

Most Americans idealise President Kennedy and demonise President Johnson, primarily because of Kennedy's untimely death and because of riots and protests in the black ghettos and over the Vietnam War under Johnson. Some Kennedy supporters contend that while Kennedy 'really cared' about blacks, Johnson was only helpful for political advantage. This chapter investigates which was the more admirable and successful president with regard to American race relations. It weighs up the importance of the presidents in the advances of the 1960s, and assesses the extent of those advances.

1 President Kennedy (1961–3)

> **KEY ISSUE** Why, when and how much did Kennedy help blacks?

a) The Kennedy Inheritance

John Kennedy knew what it was like to suffer discrimination for ethnicity. When he was 12 years old, his wealthy Boston Irish family moved to New York to escape snubbing by upper-class Bostonians of Anglo-Saxon ancestry. The Kennedys' experience of discrimination did not make them embrace blacks as brothers. One friend 'never saw a Negro on level social terms with the Kennedys. And I never heard the subject mentioned.' John's brother Robert admitted years later that, before 1961, 'I didn't lose much sleep about Negroes, I didn't think about them much, I didn't know about all the injustice.'

As a senator, John Kennedy considered it politically advantageous to oppose Eisenhower's civil rights bill. However, as civil rights became a more prominent national issue, Kennedy's interest increased proportionately. Although he employed a black secretary and two black attorneys as advisers, some blacks regarded him with suspicion and hostility. In his campaign speeches, Kennedy promised to help blacks, if he was elected president. He said discrimination in housing could be ended by a stroke of the president's pen. He said racism was immoral and damaged America's international image. Eisenhower believed that Kennedy's sympathetic phone call to Coretta King when her husband was imprisoned gained him black votes that helped him win the election. Historians disagree over whether the phone call was politically motivated or a gesture of spontaneous decency. The Democrats certainly publicised it amongst American blacks.

The new president inherited a nation with great inequalities. In 1960 most Southern blacks lacked the vote and suffered segregated housing, schools, transport and other public facilities. The great majority of Southern politicians were committed to the status quo. Some white racists used violence to prevent change. Other whites were disinclined to stop them. Southern blacks were politically, legally, economically and socially inferior. Northern blacks were in ghettos. Banks, realtors and property owners excluded them from better housing because property values plummeted when blacks moved into an area. Whites simply did not want to live alongside blacks. The 1960 Civil Rights Commission report adjudged 57% of black housing substandard. Black life expectancy was seven years less than that for whites. The black infant mortality rate was twice that for whites.

How could a president help blacks? He could get Congress to pass legislation, use his executive authority, and make symbolic appointments and gestures. Despite his campaign assurances that he would move quickly on civil rights issues, President Kennedy did not propose civil rights legislation in 1961. Why? He had no great popular mandate for action. His presidential election victory had been by the narrowest of margins. Opinion polls showed most American voters believed integration should evolve gradually, rather than be enforced by federal action. One poll showed civil rights at the bottom of the list of voter concerns. Civil rights legislation would therefore be unpopular with most voters, and also with Congress, which contained many influential Southerners. Furthermore, Kennedy planned legislation for better health care and wages for the poor. If he pushed civil rights

and alienated Southern congressmen, his whole legislative programme might suffer. If Kennedy failed to promote civil rights, black
Americans would at least benefit from other legislation. Kennedy
could also help in other ways.

b) How Kennedy Helped Blacks

One way in which historians assess Kennedy's commitment to racial
equality is by studying his appointments to office. He appointed
Harris Wofford (Howard's first white graduate) as White House civil
rights advisor, but Wofford always felt like an outsider. Roy Wilkins
wryly noted that Kennedy put so much pressure on the civil service to
employ blacks, 'that everyone was scrambling around trying to find
themselves a Negro in order to keep the president off his neck.'
Kennedy was shocked to learn how few blacks were employed in
important positions by the federal government. The FBI, for example,
had 13,649 employees, of whom only 48 were black – and they were
mostly chauffeurs. No previous president made so many black
appointments to the federal bureaucracy (it was not simply prejudice
– blacks often lacked the necessary education and experience).
Kennedy appointed 40 blacks to top posts, such as associate White
House press secretary. He chose five black federal judges, including
Thurgood Marshall. On the other hand, 20% of his Deep South judi-
cial appointments were segregationists, one of whom had referred to
black litigants as 'niggers' and 'chimpanzees', and unlawfully
obstructed black voting registration drives in Mississippi. Why did
Kennedy appoint segregationists? It was difficult to do otherwise
down South. Kennedy had to balance morality and practicality. He
had no desire to alienate Southern white voters.

Kennedy's Department of Justice had responsibility for civil rights.
The president appointed his brother Robert as Attorney General
(head of the Justice Department). The Justice Department could
quietly seek compliance with civil rights laws and court orders. John
Kennedy believed that a legalistic approach would be the least emotive and most productive way forward. The Kennedys brought 57 suits
against illegal violations of black voting rights in the South, compared
to six under Eisenhower. When Attorney General Kennedy threatened Louisiana officials with contempt of court sentences when they
denied funds to newly desegregated schools in New Orleans, it has-
tened desegregation in New Orleans, Atlanta and Memphis. On the
other hand, the Kennedy Justice Department remained cautious. It
backed down on voting rights in Mississippi when influential
Democratic senators protested (summer 1963).

Symbolic gestures were the easiest and most politically painless way
for President Kennedy to give the impression that he was committed
to racial equality. He invited more blacks to the White House than any
previous president. He might have rejected their requests for legis-

lation, but according to Wilkins, 'everyone went out of there absolutely charmed by the manner in which they had been turned down.' The president ostentatiously resigned from an exclusive club that refused to admit blacks. The Washington Redskins was the last great football club to refuse to hire blacks, so Kennedy said the team could no longer use its federally supported stadium. The Redskins signed three black players.

Blacks found the Kennedy administration disappointing on more substantial issues, such as equal opportunities in employment. Although Kennedy refused to endorse affirmative action (see page 126), he used his executive powers to create the Committee on Equal Employment Opportunity (CEEO). It aimed to ensure all Americans had equal employment opportunities within the government and with those who had contracts with the government. CEEO encouraged companies to hire more blacks. It had a few triumphs, for example, the integration and promotion of blacks at the Lockheed plant in Georgia. However, CEEO failed to bring about a great increase in black employment by federal agencies or companies doing business with the federal government and exaggerated its success herein. A 100% increase in black employment often meant a rise from one to two black employees! The Kennedys blamed CEEO chairman Vice-President Lyndon Johnson for the failures, but it was a difficult task (see pages 121–122). Employers frequently and rightly complained they were simply complying with demands from their workers for segregated facilities.

c) Reacting to Activists

President Kennedy had not planned extensive use of executive authority to help blacks. However, civil rights activists forced his hand, beginning with the Freedom Rides (1961) (see pages 88–89). Supreme Court decisions (1946 and 1960) prohibited segregated interstate buses and bus terminals. CORE aimed to provoke the Southern authorities into arresting the Freedom Riders. That would attract international attention and embarrass Kennedy's Justice Department into enforcement of the Supreme Court legislation.

White racist responses to the Freedom Riders gained national attention, especially when a white mob poured then lit kerosene on a black Freedom Rider in Montgomery. Kennedy was reluctant to intervene. He accused the Freedom Riders of lacking patriotism for having drawn attention to American domestic problems during a crisis with the Soviets. Attorney General Robert Kennedy wanted to protect the constitutional rights of the activists, but did not want to alienate Southern Democrats or the 63% of Americans who, opinion polls indicated, opposed the Freedom Rides. When Robert Kennedy's federal marshals could not control a white mob bombing a meeting at Ralph Abernathy's church, Kennedy pressured Alabama's governor to call out the National Guard and state troopers.

The Freedom Riders would not give up. Their pressure forced Robert Kennedy to get an Interstate Commerce Commission ruling that terminals and interstate bus seating should be integrated. This was supposedly achieved by autumn 1961, although a Canadian historian records seeing *de facto* segregation in the Selma, Alabama, bus station as late as 1966.[1] Although black activists had to force the administration into action, the administration had done quite well.

Later in 1961, SNCC concentrated on Southern black voter registration. The Kennedys did nothing when white racists attacked those registering to vote. Robert Kennedy condemned the violence but said the national government could not interfere with local law enforcement unless there was a total breakdown of law and order:

> Mississippi is going to work itself out.... Maybe it's going to take a decade and maybe a lot of people are going to be killed in the meantime.... But in the long run I think it's for the health of the country and the stability of the system.[2]

Robert Kennedy's cautious approach to civil rights contrasts with his war against organised crime, wherein he frequently over-reached his authority. If he was not worried about exceeding his authority, why was he so reluctant to interfere with Southern justice? The president felt SNCC 'sons of bitches' were unnecessarily provocative: 'SNCC has got an investment in violence'. The Justice Department lacked sufficient staff, and the Kennedys feared using force down South. Their inaction alienated blacks, and increased black militancy. The administration's neutral stance over the arrests of activists in Albany (see pages 89–90) also caused black criticism.

Blacks were greatly disappointed by Kennedy's record on legislation, segregationist judges, and segregated schools. It took black activism to force the administration into action again, in September 1962. Twenty-eight years old James Meredith, grandson of a slave and son of a sharecropper, had served in the Air Force for a decade. He now wanted a university education. His local black college had only one PhD on its faculty so Meredith applied for the white University of Mississippi, which did not want him. When Meredith got legal aid from the NAACP and a Supreme Court decision in his favour, Robert Kennedy had to send 500 marshals to help him enrol. The ill-equipped marshals clashed with a racist mob. Two people were shot and one third of the marshals were injured. President Kennedy had to federalise the Mississippi National Guard and order US Army regulars to the area. Meredith finally enrolled. Historians disagree over whether the administration handled the crisis well. They 'had been extremely lucky that none of the marshals had been killed, and that Meredith had not been lynched', according to Hugh Brogan.[3] On the other hand, Meredith's enrolment encouraged other blacks to do likewise.

Birmingham, Alabama, erupted next (see pages 90–93). Only Birmingham's interstate transport terminals were integrated. Other public facilities remained segregated, and black job opportunities were poor. Dr Martin Luther King Jr. organised sit-ins in downtown stores, street marches and pray-ins. When Bull Connor turned his hoses on protesters, President Kennedy said the television pictures sickened him and that he could 'well understand' black exasperation. Robert Kennedy sent in Justice Department representatives whom Andrew Young later acknowledged to have done a 'tremendous' job in bringing both sides together in preparation for change. Birmingham's public facilities were soon desegregated and black employment prospects improved. The Kennedy administration had helped greatly, albeit reluctantly at first.

Alabama was the last state to begin university integration. 'Most of us know the Southern cause is doomed,' said one congressman, 'and it is ridiculous to keep spouting defiance.' Kennedy sent in federal troops, marshals and the federalised Alabama National Guard. Governor George Wallace made a gesture of protest and then gave in, having proved his racist credentials to white voters. Kennedy made a successful and popular speech on civil rights. King was delighted that Kennedy finally admitted that this was 'primarily' a 'moral issue':

> 1 It is as old as the Scriptures and is as clear as the American Constitution. The heart of the question is whether all Americans are to be afforded equal rights and equal opportunities, whether we are going to treat our fellow Americans as we want to be treated. If an American,
> 5 because his skin is dark, cannot eat lunch in a restaurant open to the public, if he cannot send his children to the best school available, if he can not vote for the public officials who represent him, if, in short, he cannot enjoy the full and free life which all of us want, then who among us would be content to have the colour of his skin changed and stand
> 10 in his place? Who among us would then be content with the counsels of patience and delay?[4]

As usual, Kennedy had been prodded into action. However, as so often, his administration contributed to a satisfactory solution.

In summer 1963 Kennedy opposed the proposed Washington March (see pages 93–94). He considered it a rebuke for his slowness over civil rights. He feared it would antagonise Congress and jeopardise his civil rights bill (see pages 116–117). 'I don't want to give any of them a chance to say, "Yes, I'm for the bill, but I'm damned if I'll vote for it at the point of a gun"'. However, Kennedy eventually endorsed the march, and worked hard to make it interracial, peaceful and supportive of the bill. Critics consequently charged the administration with taking over the march. Malcolm X christened it 'The Farce on Washington'. Some historians claim Kennedy aides were ready to 'pull the plug' on the public address system if hostile words were spoken against the administration. That proved unnecessary. The march was a great success and facilitated the passage of the civil rights bill.

There is no doubt that black activism pushed Kennedy further and faster than he had intended. The civil rights movement was more important than the president was in initiating change.

d) Legislation

Although Kennedy promised in his presidential election campaign that discrimination in housing could be ended at a 'stroke of the presidential pen', he did nothing initially. Disappointed blacks inundated the president with pens to jog his memory. Why did Kennedy do nothing? He thought that if he pushed legislation on this issue, Congress would reject both his Department of Urban Affairs bill (they did anyway) and his appointment of the first black Cabinet member. Also, with the congressional elections of 1962 looming, Northern Democratic Congressmen did not want their white voters upset by the thought of living next door to blacks. After those elections, Kennedy introduced a half-hearted measure that only applied to future federal housing. It was certainly difficult to obtain congressional co-operation. For example, the 1962 administration literacy bill enabling blacks with a sixth grade education to vote, failed because of a Southern filibuster.

Kennedy took a long time to ask Congress for a major civil rights law, maintaining that a Southern filibuster would surely overcome it. Why then did Kennedy finally propose a civil rights bill? He was disappointed that businessmen and local authorities were slow to respond to his pleas to employ blacks and desegregate public facilities. He was also influenced by increasing Southern violence, and by criticism from civil rights activists. Birmingham was a vivid and stimulating reminder of the issues (see pages 90–93). Birmingham forced Kennedy to respond, as he admitted. Was his response purely political? There was probably some element of sympathy and idealism. He himself had suffered bigoted comments about his religion and ethnicity in the presidential election campaign. Kennedy read books like J. K. Galbraith's *The Affluent Society* (1958) which drew attention to the great disparity in wealth and opportunity in America.

Kennedy knew it would be hard to get congressional co-operation. 'A good many programmes I care about may go down the drain as a result of this – we may all go down the drain.' So, his proposed bill (February 1963) was a moderate attempt to guarantee desegregation in public places and help blacks to use their vote. The bill helped black workers, although civil rights activists felt that would be of limited usefulness without an FEPC (see pages 47–49). The bill got stuck in Congress, partly because liberal 'sons of bitches' (Robert Kennedy) tried to push it too far for Republicans. It is difficult to decide whether the bill became an act in the next administration because of sadness over Kennedy's assassination, because of Kennedy's efforts with congressmen, or because of President

Johnson (see page 123). John Lewis of CORE said it was 'too little, too late'. However, it was a start. It certainly did more for blacks than Eisenhower's legislation.

e) Conclusion

What had Kennedy achieved? While appointments such as Thurgood Marshall encouraged blacks, Kennedy had also appointed segregationist judges. The administration had given some help to black voters. It helped get the 24th Amendment (which stopped the poll tax) and Johnson's Civil Rights Act (1964). However, it took Johnson's 1965 Voting Right Act to ensure blacks could exercise their right to vote. Kennedy made several gestures that publicised his commitment to racial equality at little or no cost. While his CEEO achieved little, its existence at least reminded employers of their obligations.

Black activists pushed the reluctant administration into action on several occasions. As a result, the administration's intervention in Southern states was unprecedented. They used federal force and injunctions to get interstate buses and terminals and universities desegregated. They played a part in obtaining the Birmingham agreement. However, civil rights activists felt that Kennedy was a great disappointment. Sometimes, as with Albany and SNCC voter registration efforts, the administration remained steadfastly unhelpful. Kennedy was slow to issue an Executive Order desegregating federally supported housing.

Kennedy was slow in promoting change, calculating that slowness made change more acceptable. Polls show just how politically risky Kennedy's actions were. A September 1963 poll showed 89% of blacks approved of his presidency, but 70% of Southern whites felt he was moving too fast on integration. 50% of Americans agreed with that. Kennedy's approval rating in the South dropped from 60% in March 1963, to 44% in September 1963. He had probably gone as far as he could go. Southerners in Congress were becoming uncooperative over all administration legislation. The civil rights bill moved very slowly. Southern whites were very resentful of Kennedy's changes. There was still much violence in the South, as in the church bombing which killed four children in Birmingham, Alabama. A white backlash against the civil rights movement had begun in the North.

At last, in response to black pressure, Kennedy had morally committed the presidency to reform. This damaged his Democratic Party in the South, as he knew it would. It takes considerable courage for a politician to compromise his own party and his own presidential re-election prospects. Kennedy and his successor Johnson both risked this and could perhaps both be called genuine statesmen rather than mere politicians in their commitment to black equality.

2 Lyndon Johnson – Teacher, New Dealer, Congressman and Senator

> KEY ISSUES How do Johnson's life and career illustrate racial politics? To what extent was he motivated by political advantage? How much did Johnson contribute to racial equality?

Lyndon Johnson's reputation has been badly tarnished by 'his' Vietnam War. However, a recent biographer suggests:

Johnson's role in reaching out to America's disadvantaged and combating racial segregation was perhaps his most important contribution to recent US history.[5]

a) Johnson's Early Career

Some people believe Johnson was nothing more than an unprincipled politician. However, he claimed to be an idealist who wanted to make America a better and fairer place for its inhabitants. A study of Johnson's words and deeds should help you decide for yourself.

Johnson's work for minorities began in 1928 with his first job as an elementary school teacher in what he described as 'one of the crummiest little towns in Texas'. The segregated school contained only Mexican Americans. Johnson recalled his 28 pupils as 'mired in the slums', 'lashed by prejudice', 'buried half-alive in illiteracy'. Johnson believed that education would be their escape route. He bribed, bullied, cajoled and encouraged his pupils. They adored him. What motivated Johnson? Idealism ran in his family. In his father's short career in the Texas state legislature, he bravely opposed 'Ku Klux sons of bitches'. Johnson was motivated by memories of his own childhood poverty and by his belief that giving help to minorities would bring spiritual and economic benefit to all Americans. He believed racial discrimination damaged the economy of his beloved South. He was ambitious, but also caring and compassionate. 'I wanted power to give things to people ... especially the poor and the blacks.'

During the Depression (see page 40) Johnson worked for a New Deal Agency, the National Youth Administration. Johnson was horrified when Washington ordered him to have a black leader as a close advisor. Johnson said he would be 'run out of Texas' if he implemented this. He explained why reform had to be slow:

1 The racial question during the last 100 years in Texas ... has resolved itself into a definite system of mores and customs which cannot be upset overnight. So long as these are observed there is harmony and peace between the races in Texas [15% black, 12% Hispanic]. But it is exceed-
5 ingly difficult to step over lines so long established and to upset customs so deep-rooted, by any act which is so shockingly against precedent as the attempt to mix Negroes and whites on a common board.[6]

Johnson made great efforts to alleviate black unemployment (nearly 50% in 1932). Although he privately referred to blacks as 'niggers', he sometimes slept at black colleges to see how NYA was working, and blacks thought him unusually helpful. However, Johnson and NYA did little for Hispanics. Why? There was no political pressure from Washington to help Hispanics, especially as many Texas Mexicans were not American citizens. Also, Johnson believed that because their landlords helped them, Mexicans were better equipped to survive the Depression than blacks.

When Johnson became a congressman, he wanted the minority vote, so he considered employing 'a talented and good-looking Mexican' or a Spanish-American girl as a secretary to show his 'appreciation' of his Mexican supporters. In 1949, a segregated Texas cemetery would not bury a Mexican American war hero. Johnson therefore arranged a burial in Arlington National Cemetery, thereby gaining front-page praise in the *New York Times*. Some white Texans interpreted that as a cynical publicity stunt. Was it? Any Texan who sought to represent that segregated state had to appear to be a segregationist. It took courage to make gestures such as this. On the other hand, it was an easy way to win minority votes, and it made a politician with national ambitions look free from sectional prejudices.

As black voters were relatively few, political expediency dictated that Johnson vote with his fellow Southern Democrats in Congress against civil rights measures which aimed to prevent lynching, eliminate poll taxes and deny federal funding to segregated schools. Senator Johnson's opposition to Truman's civil rights programme disgusted Texas blacks. His explanations (or excuses) are valid (if not admirable) within the contemporary Southern political context. He said the bills would never have passed anyway. As he pointed out, 'There is nothing more useless than a dead liberal.' He thought he might be more helpful later, in some other place and position. He recognised that he could only 'go so far in Texas'. He also trotted out the standard Southerner's excuse for refusal to help blacks. He said he was not against blacks but for states' rights. He thought civil rights legislation which tried 'to force people to do what they are not ready to do of their own free will and accord' would lead to a 'wave of riots' across the South. Finally, like Booker T. Washington, Johnson argued that civil rights legislation would not help blacks and Hispanics as much as better housing, schooling and healthcare. Behind-the-scenes, where white voters could not see, Johnson worked to get black farmers and black schoolchildren equal treatment in his congressional district. In 1938 he managed to get federal funding for housing in Austin, Texas, which benefited Mexicans, blacks, and white slum dwellers. He appealed to white self-interest when he told the press,

This country won't have to worry about isms [communism and fascism] when it gives its people a decent, clean place to live and a job. They'll believe in the government. They'll be ready to fight for it.[7]

The need to keep in with voters of all colours, coupled with his own idealism and racial ambivalence, made Johnson appear a Jekyll and Hyde figure on race relations. From the mid-1940s, Robert Parker worked for Johnson as a part-time servant as private dinner parties in Washington. Parker recalled it as a 'painful experience'. He feared,

1   the pain and humiliation he could inflict at a moment's notice.... In front of his guests Johnson would often 'nigger' at me. He especially liked to put on a show for [Mississippi] Senator Bilbo, who used to lecture: 'the only way to treat in nigger is to kick him' ... I used to dread
5   being around Johnson when Bilbo was present, because I knew it meant that Johnson would play racist. That was the LBJ I hated. Privately, he was a different man as long as I didn't do anything to make him angry. He'd call me 'boy' almost affectionately. Sometimes I felt that he was
10 treating me almost as an equal.... Although I never heard him speak publicly about black men without saying 'nigger,' I never heard him say 'nigger woman.' In fact, he always used to call his black cook, Zephyr Wright, a college graduate who couldn't find any other work, 'Miss Wright' or 'sweetheart.'[8]

By the mid-1950s, Senator Johnson appeared to be changing his position on civil rights issues. He was one of the few Southern politicians who supported the Supreme Court's BROWN decision. Why? He said it was important to uphold the American Constitution and the Supreme Court's place within it. 'However we may question the judgement,' it 'cannot be overruled now'. He felt a great debate about BROWN would only weaken the Democrats and the country. He wanted the South to accept it, believing that the South had to accept desegregation in order to make economic advances. He knew racial tensions made the South unattractive to investors. His presidential ambitions meant that he could not be seen to be too narrowly Southern, which helps explain why he was one of the three Southern senators who refused to sign the Southern Manifesto against BROWN. As always, Johnson's motivation was and is debatable. While one senator described it as 'one of the most courageous acts of political valour I have ever seen', Hubert Humphrey said Johnson was 'very proud' of his stance and 'used it' for political gain, hoping thereby to win Northern black and white voters.

    Johnson remained careful to appease Southern racists. In 1956 he killed a civil rights bill in Congress, but changed his position in 1957. While assuring Texans there was 'no foundation' to rumours that he was promoting a civil rights bill, and that he was 'strongly and irrevocably opposed to forced integration of the races', he orchestrated the passage of the 1957 Civil Rights Act. However, he diluted the parts most offensive to Southerners. He turned Eisenhower's bill into a largely unenforceable (because of white domination of Southern juries) voting rights law. The part that allowed the federal government to promote integration in Southern schools was lost.

Nevertheless the bill symbolised greater federal interest in and protection of black rights. Johnson was also very important in the passage of Eisenhower's second Civil Rights Act.

Why did Johnson suddenly promote civil rights legislation? He hoped it would show his talent for creating consensus. He needed some dramatic legislative achievement if he was to become a serious presidential candidate. He did not want to be seen as a sectional politician, a conservative Southerner. How better to prove he could rise above narrow sectionalism than by promoting civil rights legislation? Northern black voters were beginning to switch to the Republicans, so the issue was increasingly important to Johnson and the Democrats. A friend told Johnson he could impress everyone, by telling Northerners he was fighting for a stronger bill, and Southerners that he was trying to dilute the bill! The time was ripe for change, following the Montgomery bus boycott and BROWN. If change was inevitable, it made sense to go along with it. Johnson believed the future of the South depended on the decrease of racial strife. Many of those close to Johnson said he had a genuine sympathy for greater racial equality, even though he talked in 'good ole boy' language to other Southerners.

b) Vice-President Johnson (1961–3)

While Johnson was Kennedy's Vice-President, racism became an increasingly important political issue. Johnson attempted to explain racism:

> I'll tell you what's at the bottom of it. If you can convince the lowest white man that he's better than the best coloured man, he won't notice you picking his pocket. Hell, give him somebody to look down on, and he'll empty his pockets for you.[9]

However, Johnson knew something had to be done about it:

> The Negro fought in the war [World War Two], and ... he's not gonna keep taking the shit we're dishing out. We're in a race with time. If we don't act, we're gonna have blood in the streets.[10]

Vice-President Johnson's greatest challenge was chairing Kennedy's Committee on Equal Employment Opportunity (CEEO). Johnson did not want the job. He knew Kennedy was passing him a hot potato. He told Kennedy CEEO lacked the necessary money and power. However, when Kennedy insisted, Johnson, as always, did his best. Why? Johnson believed America was 'just throwing aside one of our greatest assets' ('brain power') because of racism. Johnson considered discrimination un-American'. It damaged America's reputation. James Farmer believed Johnson's motivation was genuine, not political. Farmer and Roy Wilkins both rated Vice-President Johnson higher than President Kennedy on civil rights issues. However, CEEO

failed to win many plaudits. Johnson had to take care not to push con-
tractors too far and too fast on equal employment, lest it damage him
and the administration. Federal jobs held by blacks increased by 17%
in 1962 and 22% in 1963 but black activists were still dissatisfied. They
wanted decreased black unemployment and comprehensive civil
rights legislation.

Shortly before Kennedy's assassination, Vice-President Johnson
urged the administration to make a real 'moral commitment' to civil
rights. The tone in his recorded phone call suggests Johnson might
have been the one who 'really cared' about civil rights.

1963 – STATISTICS

Total US population – 189,242,000; Black population –
20,000,000; Hispanic population – 572,564. White unemployment
– 5%; Non-white unemployment – 10%.

---

3 President Johnson

> **KEY ISSUES** How much did Johnson contribute to racial equality?
> Who and what helped and hindered him? What motivated him?

a) The 1964 Civil Rights Act

Lyndon Johnson became president after Kennedy's assassination. He
announced his vision of a 'Great Society' for America, with 'an end to
poverty and racial injustice'. He was determined to get Kennedy's civil
rights bill through. When a Southern senator told him the price
would be the presidential election, Johnson said, 'I'll pay it gladly'.
Why did Johnson stake his all on the bill? He told people discrimination was morally wrong, and described how, when his black cook
drove to Texas, she could not use the whites-only facilities in a gas
station:

> When they had to go to the bathroom, they would ... pull off on a side
> road, and Zephyr Wright, the cook of the vice-president of the United
> States, would squat in the road to pee. That's wrong. And there ought
> to be something to change that.[11]

He remained convinced that reform would help the economic, political and spiritual reintegration of the South within the nation. Also,
as a non-elected president, he felt duty-bound to see the late president's bill through. His sense of obligation was increased by the tragic
circumstances of Kennedy's death. Why had it taken Johnson so long
to become a staunch civil rights advocate? He told Roy Wilkins he was
'free at last': as president he could put the national interest above
narrow sectional interests. Wilkins believed Johnson was 'absolutely

sincere'. Would the Civil Rights Act help or hinder Johnson in his campaign for re-election in 1964? Andrew Young said while it was 'the way to really save the nation, he knew it was not politically expedient'. On the other hand, it ensured that he won most black votes.

How was the bill passed? Black activists had drawn the attention of the nation and its legislators to injustices. 'The real hero of this struggle is the American Negro,' said Johnson. However, there were doubters in Congress. The bill had to overcome the longest filibuster in Senate history. Its passage owed much to Kennedy, who had won over the Republican minority leader before his death. Other important congressional leaders like Hubert Humphrey deserve credit. Johnson thought the bill would have passed if Kennedy had lived, but it might have been emasculated like Eisenhower's bills. Now Johnson did not have to compromise the bill's contents. A Johnson aide gave the credit for the passage of the bill to Johnson himself. He devoted a staggering amount of his time, energy, and political capital to breaking the Senate filibuster and ensuring the passage of the act. Johnson made emotive appeals: he said a civil rights act would be Kennedy's best 'eulogy'. Furthermore, he appealed to national traditions and ideals. 'We have talked long enough in this country about equal rights.' Now it was time for it to be enshrined in law. He tried to win over Southerners by appealing to their self-interest. He emphasised how the bill would help get blacks and Hispanics working:

> I'm gonna try to teach these nigras that don't know anything how to work for themselves instead of just breedin'; I'm gonna try to teach these Mexicans who can't talk English to learn it so they can work for themselves ... and get off of our taxpayer's back.[12]

A final factor in the passage of the act was increasing nationwide support: by January 1964, 68% of Americans favoured the bill. After Birmingham, national religious organisations had increasingly supported the measure. Congress could not afford to ignore this marked swing in public opinion.

Johnson signed the civil rights bill in July 1964 before a national TV audience. He spoke movingly of the millions deprived of equality:

> The reasons are deeply imbedded in history and tradition and the nature of man. We can understand – without rancour or hatred – how this happened, but it cannot continue.... Our Constitution, the foundation of our Republic, forbids it. The principles of our freedom forbid it. Morality forbids it. And the law I will sign tonight forbids it.[13]

What was the significance of the Civil Rights Act? Irving Bernstein described it as 'a rare and glittering moment in the history of American democracy'.[14] The act gave the federal government the legal tools to end *de jure* segregation in the South. It prohibited discrimination in public places, furthered school desegregation, and established an Equal Employment Commission. However, it did little to facilitate black voting, and little to improve race relations. There were signs of a Northern working-class white backlash in the popularity of Alabama's racist Governor George Wallace in presidential primaries. Blacks felt the act had not gone far enough. They still suffered from poverty and discrimination. The weeks following the passage of the act saw riots in the black ghettos of many East Coast cities. Furthermore, the predominantly black Mississippi Freedom Democratic Party demanded seats at the Democratic party convention in Atlantic City, New Jersey, on the basis that they were more representative than the segregationists who represented Mississippi. Johnson was outraged. He told a friend he thought the act would cost him politically: 'we just delivered the South to the Republican Party for a long time to come'. That was true. He felt he had done a great deal to help blacks and now black activists sought to repay him with demonstrations that would embarrass him and the party.

Johnson's plan was to continue to try to help but in his own way and at his own speed. In an effective and popular campaign speech in New Orleans, for example, Johnson courageously gambled on speaking the truth about the South being held back economically and politically by racism. He also planned further legislation.

b) Johnson's Legislation

Johnson hoped that his Elementary and Secondary Education Act (1965) would help children out of the ghettos. Poorer states like Mississippi benefited greatly from the federal funding. By the end of the 1960s, the percentage of blacks who had a high school diploma increased from 40% to 60%. However, a combination of reluctant local officials, and ghetto peer pressure and traditions, limited the act's effectiveness. His Higher Education Act (1965) was more successful. It gave significant aid to poor black colleges. The number of black college students quadrupled within a decade. Similarly, Johnson's introduction of Medicare and Medicaid helped poor minorities: the black infant mortality rate halved within a decade.

There were gaps in the 1964 Civil Rights Act that needed filling, but Johnson feared uncooperative Southerners in Congress. However, King's campaign to register black voters in Selma, Alabama (see pages 96–98) made Johnson remind Americans that one individual's loss of the right to vote 'undermines the freedom of every citizen.' Then 'Bloody Sunday' forced Johnson to ask Congress for the voting rights bill.

Johnson's persuasive speech before Congress was one of his best:

ı Rarely are we met with a challenge ... to the values and the purposes and the meaning of our beloved Nation. The issue of equal rights for American Negroes is such an issue.... The command of the Constitution is plain.... It is wrong – deadly wrong – to deny any of
5 your fellow Americans the right to vote in this country.... A century

has passed, more than a hundred years, since the Negro was freed. And he is not fully free tonight.... A century has passed, more than a hundred years, since equality was promised. And yet the Negro is not equal.... The real hero of this struggle is the American Negro. His
10 actions and protests, his courage to risk safety and even to risk his life, have awakened the conscience of this Nation.... He has called upon us to make good the promise of America. And who among us can say that we would have made the same progress were it not for his persistent bravery, and his faith in American democracy?[15]

Martin Luther King said the speech brought tears to his eyes.

Johnson's Voting Rights Act outlawed literacy tests and poll taxes. It had a dramatic effect on the South. By late 1966, only four of the old Confederate states had fewer than 50% of their eligible blacks registered. By 1968, even Mississippi was up to 59%. In 1980, the proportion of blacks registered to vote was only 7% less than the proportion of whites. Blacks elected to office in the South increased dramatically. Their numbers increased six-fold 1965–9, then doubled 1969–80. There was political gain for Johnson's Democratic Party. The enlarged black vote helped counter the loss of Southern white voters for the Democratic Party.

For reasons discussed below, it grew harder to obtain reforming acts. A 1968 Civil Rights Act prohibited discrimination in the sale or rental of housing, but little more was done to help blacks. Nevertheless, from 1964–5, Johnson had engineered a legislative revolution. How? It was a 'unique set of circumstances', according to one biographer.[16] Due to his 24 years in Congress, for many of which he was Democratic Party leader, Johnson had unprecedented experience in getting legislation through Congress. He had an unusual two-thirds of Congress on his side (it is rare to have both a Democratic majority in Congress and a Democratic President). Congressmen knew their constituents were unusually receptive at this time to righting national wrongs, partly because they felt it would somehow atone for Kennedy's death. Finally, and most important of all, the president was exceptionally persuasive and determined, and had a lifelong commitment to helping the poor.

c) Johnson and Executive Authority

Johnson, like Kennedy, used executive authority to help blacks. In 1965–6 Johnson worked to help blacks through manipulation of federal funding, for example, offering federal subsidies to Southern districts which were cooperative on school desegregation. By September 1965 there was 88% compliance down South. The numbers of black students attending desegregated schools tripled. Johnson used black advisers, including future Congresswoman Barbara Jordan. A Supreme Court vacancy in 1967 gave Johnson the opportunity to make an appointment to help black morale. Every Supreme Court judge in 178 years of the nation's existence had been a white male. Lady Bird Johnson suggested her husband should appoint the first woman, but he appointed the first black. There had been no great civil rights advance in nearly two years, and Congress seemed unlikely to pass any helpful legislation. The appointment of a black justice would help to counter the image of lawless black rioters. Johnson therefore appointed 58 year-old Thurgood Marshall.

The son of a railroad worker and kindergarten teacher, Marshall had grown up in Baltimore, Maryland, which he said was as segregated as any Southern city. Blacks could not attend the University of Maryland, so he went to Howard University. He began his legal career with NAACP in 1936. He won cases relating to equality in house sales, voting, and teacher salaries. His most famous victory was against segregated education in BROWN (1954). In 1961 Kennedy made him a judge of the US Court of Appeals. In 1965 Johnson made him Solicitor General, then in 1967, Supreme Court justice. Johnson told a journalist that although he would probably suffer politically (again!) Marshall's appointment would inspire all black people. Southern senators opposed the appointment, but on constitutional not racial grounds (they claimed Marshall was too liberal). Johnson got some hostile mail. 'You despicable bum. How do you have the guts to do it coming out of Texas?' asked one bigot who, like many other whites, felt Johnson had done more than enough for blacks.

Johnson knew that legislation alone could not ensure equality. As he told university students at Howard University, in 1965,

1 You do not take a person who, for years, has been hobbled by chains
   and liberate him, bring him up to the starting line of a race and then say,
   'you are free to compete with all the others,' and still justly believe that
   you have been completely fair.... This is the next and the more pro-
5 found stage of the battle for civil rights.[17]

Johnson said what was needed was positive discrimination to help blacks (this became known as 'affirmative action'). However, Johnson's plans to help blacks further were hit by the great white backlash after riots in Watts, Los Angeles (August 1965).

d) Ghetto Riots and the White Backlash

Watts had palm tree-lined, litter free streets, and small, neat homes, but also had high levels of unemployment and crime. The riots demonstrated universal black discontent. Blacks suffered *de facto* segregation and discrimination that was all the more frustrating because it was unspoken and therefore difficult to legislate against. Out of half a million blacks in south central Los Angeles, an estimated 10–80,000 had rioted. Many of the rioters were young black males. Their targets included expensive stores and middle class blacks. What were the results and significance of the Watts riots? Thirty-four died and $35 million worth of property was damaged. The riots caused a white backlash. What else could be expected, asked Los Angeles' police chief, 'when you keep telling people they are unfairly treated and teach them disrespect for the law'? Throughout California, gun sales to suburban whites soared. Anxious whites throughout America now turned against blacks and against Johnson's reform programme. Whites were tired of taking the blame for the black predicament. Johnson at first could not believe what was happening in Watts. 'How is it possible, after all we've accomplished?' He was amazed and disappointed by what he later described as 'all that crazy rioting which almost ruined everything'. Johnson could not understand how black militants could be so politically naive. Could they not see how their behaviour undermined his efforts to get public and congressional support for more legislation? How could they be so unappreciative of what he had done? Johnson secretly arranged that federal funds be poured into Watts but publicly he likened the black rioters to the Ku Klux Klan. He wanted to avoid accusations that his sympathetic policies encouraged rioters to demand more. Johnson told a colleague his fears:

1 Negroes will end up pissing in the aisles of the Senate ... [and] making fools of themselves the way ... they had after the Civil War and during Reconstruction. Just as the government was moving to help them, the Negroes will once again take unwise actions out of frustration, impa-
5 tience and anger.[18]

Fearful of the white backlash, the administration kept a lower profile on race issues. Johnson made heavy weather of appointing the first black cabinet member. Vice-President Hubert Humphrey was removed from the chairmanship of the President's Council on Equal Opportunity. In all these actions, Johnson tried to make it clear that black extremism would make his administration less rather than more helpful. Johnson concentrated instead on his 'Great Society' programmes that helped the poor ethnic minorities.

e) What Stopped Johnson Doing More?

Johnson had done more for blacks than any other president had, but after 1965 it became hard to do more. Why? Firstly, Congress was awkward. In January 1966, for example, Johnson proposed a 'demonstration cities' bill to try to arrest urban blight in leading cities. Congressional conservatives opposed the bill as 'something for blacks'. Some said black power advocates would dominate its implementation, and it would result in school busing. The bill only scraped through Congress by a narrow margin. In 1965 Congress rejected an administration civil rights bill, one aim of which was to prohibit housing discrimination. Many congressmen opposed an end to discrimination in housing sales and rentals, as their white constituents did not want the drop in property values which followed integrated housing. Johnson appealed in vain to their self-interest:

> Minorities have been artificially compressed into ghettos where unemployment and ignorance are rampant, where human tragedies and crime abound, and where city administrations are burdened with rising social costs and falling tax revenues.[19]

Congress remained unenthusiastic. Polls showed 70% of white Americans opposed large numbers of blacks living in their neighbourhood, especially after the Watts riots and Stokely Carmichael's call for 'black power'. Johnson's proposed bill resulted in some of the worst hate mail of his presidency. When housing discrimination was finally prohibited in a 1968 act, the law proved difficult to enforce due to white resistance. Johnson found it hard to sustain national and congressional support for his war on poverty. He was angry with congressmen who jokingly called his rat extermination bill a 'civil rats bill' and who suggested he send in a federal cat army. Johnson pointed out that slum children suffered terribly from rat bites.

Secondly, Johnson had to rely on local and state authorities, officials and employees to carry out his programmes. They were sometimes reluctant to co-operate, as in Chicago. One million blacks constituted Chicago's largest ethnic group. Whites did not want to live near nor share schools with blacks. The 1964 Civil Rights Act said federal funding should not be given to segregated schools, but Mayor Daley was a valuable political ally, so he got his funds and kept his segregated schools. This pattern was repeated in other Northern cities.

Rioting blacks did not help Johnson's efforts on their behalf. They turned whites against his policies. Summer 1966 saw riots in 38 major cities, including Chicago, Atlanta and Philadelphia. In July 1967, amidst rumours of police brutality against a black cab driver, Newark's black ghetto erupted. In six days of riots, 26 died, 1500 were injured, and much of the inner city was burned out. Then Detroit erupted. Forty died, 2000 were injured, 5000 were arrested, and 5000 were homeless. The president had to send federal troops to settle Detroit. Inner city riots became an annual summer event. An aide counted 225 'hostile outbursts' from 1964–8, in which 191 were killed, 7942 wounded, and 49,607 arrested. What caused them? Big city ghetto residents could compare highly visible white affluence with their own situation. The FBI blamed the misery of ghetto life, oppressive summer weather, and Communist agitation. Johnson believed it was poverty and despair: while 8% of whites lived below the poverty line, 30% of blacks did so; 18% of whites lived in substandard housing, 50% of non-whites did so. Between 1959 and 1965, the number of poor Americans decreased from 39 million to 33 million, but the percentage of poor blacks increased from 28% to 31%. Black unemployment (7%) was twice that of whites. Johnson told journalists that the riots could not just have been about unemployment because there were training vacancies in most of the riot cities. In Detroit, 80% of those arrested had well paid jobs. He said it was more likely 'bad housing' and 'the hate and bitterness which has been developing over many years'. The absence of black policeman fuelled ghetto tensions against white police 'outsiders'. A subsequent analysis of ghetto riots found 40% involved alleged police abuse or discrimination. Johnson's investigatory Kerner Commission blamed white racism above all. Blacks saw the police as 'the occupying army of white America, a hostile power'. The *Boston Globe* described the 1967 Newark riots as 'a revolution of black Americans against white Americans, a violent petition for the redress of long-standing grievances'. It said Johnson's legislation had effected little fundamental improvement. Some suggest that false hopes raised by Johnson's extravagant Great Society rhetoric played a part in provoking the riots. King's assassination by a white racist provoked major riots in 100 cities, with 46 dead, 3000 injured, 27,000 arrested. 21,000 federal troops and 34,000 National Guardsmen restored order following $45 million of damage to property. What was the white response? Suburban whites feared black militants were driving America into race war. TV showed black youths shouting 'burn, burn, burn'. Whites turned hostile. A 1965 poll showed 88% of whites advocated black self-improvement, more education, and harder work, rather than government help. A 1966 poll showed 90% opposition to new civil rights legislation. In a 1967 poll, 52% said Johnson was going 'too fast' on integration, and only 10% said 'not fast enough'. Black militants also fuelled the white backlash. When CORE and SNCC expelled their white members in 1966–7, they lost white financial backing and moral support. 95% of CORE's money in 1965 came from whites, especially liberal Jews, now increasingly the target of militant black invective. When the Black Panthers talked of carrying weapons for self defence, they frightened and alienated whites. Black militancy served to destroy organisations that previously worked with whites to gain beneficial legislation. In 1968 Stokely 'Starmichael', as disillusioned SNCC members called him, took SNCC into a merger with the Black Panthers which effectively finished SNCC off.

The expense and distraction of the Vietnam War helps to explain why Johnson could not do as much as he wanted to alleviate America's domestic problems. Furthermore, Johnson recognised that he could not work miracles. In June 1966 Johnson told a task force set up to report on black problems that,

> The dilemma that you deal with is too deeply rooted in pride and prejudice, too profound and too complex, and too critical to our future for any one man or any one administration to ever resolve.[20]

He knew there was a limit to the amount of legislation that any administration could pass, particularly if most of the population were beginning to resist it. 'It's a little like whisky,' said Johnson. 'It is good. But if you drink too much it comes up on you.' 'We have come too far too fast during your administration,' a leading Democrat told him.

Which of all these factors was most important in slowing down Johnson's War on Poverty and civil rights programme? Some blamed Vietnam, some the white backlash. Federal spending on the poor had increased by nearly 50% and this helped make his programme increasingly unpopular among whites. In 1967, the Democratic governor of Missouri told Johnson that 'public disenchantment with the civil rights programmes' was one of the main reasons why he and the Democrats were so unpopular. White Americans were tired of hearing about America's oppressed minorities. The programmes were expensive and it appeared that political radicals were hijacking them.

4 Conclusions

KEY ISSUES What had Johnson achieved? Were his aims and methods realistic? Who or what bore greatest responsibility for the advances?

Johnson did not stand for re-election in 1968. Significantly, his last public appearance (against the advice of his doctors) was at a civil rights symposium. He gave his own assessment of his achievements when he said there was still a long way to go to real equality. A few weeks later he was dead. When his body lay in state in the Capitol Rotunda in Washington, around 60% of those who filed pass to pay their respects were blacks. One said, 'People don't know it, but he did more for us than anybody, any president, ever did.'

What had he achieved? He played an important role in ending *de jure* discrimination and segregation in the South. Martin Luther King's old friend Bayard Rustin found the South transformed by 1980, 'from a reactionary bastion into a region moderate in racial outlook and more enlightened in social and economic policy'. Johnson's Voting Rights Act transformed Southern politics, by giving blacks the opportunity to vote without fear. In 1960 there had been no black officials in Mississippi; by 1980 there were over 300. His Education Acts speeded up school desegregation and helped black colleges. He had been instrumental in the passage of three Civil Rights Acts that gave blacks more political and economic opportunities. His civil rights legislation opened the way for a larger and richer black middle class. Black unemployment decreased by 34% and the percentage of blacks living below the poverty line decreased by 25%. Johnson's Great Society had contributed greatly to those statistics.

On the other hand, most blacks continued to live in poor housing and to suffer above average unemployment. Great Society programmes were soon unpopular with local politicians who resented federal intervention, and with ordinary Americans who disliked the radical redistribution of resources that the programmes required to work effectively on the eradication of poverty. It was hard to get out of the poverty trap. Discrimination had a long tradition and *de facto* segregation, particularly in schools, remained in the South. The Civil Rights Act of 1968 was 'an empty gesture', according to a recent Johnson biographer. 'Enforcement was fatally defective', according to the historian Irving Bernstein.[21] Neither government departments, nor the real estate industry, nor ordinary black and white people had any real desire to make it work. Critics say the Great Society created a 'welfare dependency' culture. Federal expenditure rocketed. In 1991, a *New York Times* article said Johnson's 'demonstration cities' legislation had failed. The original plan to concentrate on a few cities to see how a reforming programme could work had been sabotaged by 'every legislator' wanting 'a slice of the pork'. The resources were spread thinly over 150 cities. On the other hand, San Francisco showed how the act raised awareness and led to progress.

Some blacks were dissatisfied with his achievements, although it has been argued that without Johnson's efforts black extremism would have gained a far larger following. Riots demonstrated some blacks' desire for more and faster progress, and this precipitated a white backlash that helped to ensure that Johnson could not do much more to help black Americans. As a politician, he was always on the lookout for votes. He did not promote desegregation in the North for fear of antagonising voters and he overruled a zealous assistant who tried to cut off federal funding to Chicago schools, because Daley was a political ally. However, while many blacks thought he had done too little, many whites thought he had done too much. Johnson's Kerner Commission Report explained the 1967 ghetto riots as a result of white racism, and recommended greater federal expenditure. That was politically unrealistic. Like Martin Luther King, Johnson probably did as much as was humanly possible in the circumstances. Both tried to improve American race relations by improving the situation of blacks, but both found it difficult to overcome the historic legacy of dislike, discrimination, and inequality.

President Eisenhower's brother described Johnson as 'the most militant civil rights leader' in American history! Ironically, those like Johnson and King, who worked for equality believing it would lead to improved race relations, actually damaged race relations. White resentment grew, while blacks understandably wanted more and faster. Would Johnson have done better not to have tried? Did his emotional overstatements on the extent of deprivation help create a mood of revolt? He probably attempted too much and he certainly achieved far less than he had wanted and promised. Once in power, the consummate politician seemed to forget political reality. Back in Texas, he knew there was only so much he could do. His visions of what he could do as president in the White House were unrealistic, but his ideals were surely admirable. Who was 'right', Kennedy who had to be pushed into minimal action or Johnson who perhaps pushed too hard? Thurgood Marshall thought Johnson got it right: 'You didn't wait for the times. You made them.'

As he left office, Johnson said, 'so little have I done. So much do I have yet to do.' Perhaps he was being too modest. His biographers have often been very generous. 'THIS PRESIDENCY MADE A DIF-FERENCE,' one insisted. 'The nation was transformed in civil rights ... education ... [and] poverty'.[22] Historians of civil rights perhaps inevitably give most of the credit elsewhere: 'African Americans were the principal architects of their own success', according to Robert Cook.[23] Perhaps progress was due to both.

The advances of this period inevitably owed much to the creation and enforcement of laws and legal decisions. Who or what was most responsible for this? Clearly, Congress had to be won over, and a study of the chronology of their legislation makes it seem as if significant deaths and violence were of great importance. The 1964 Civil Rights Act was passed only after the death of Kennedy, and the 1968 Civil Rights Act followed the assassination of Martin Luther King and riots in 126 cities. Disorder in Selma was followed by the Voting Rights Act (1965). Of the two presidents, it was obviously Johnson who had the greatest success in seeing legislation through Congress. Kennedy's biggest contribution was probably his assassination. Black leaders who orchestrated campaigns such as that for voter registration in Selma played a vital part in pushing presidents and Congress into helpful legislation and helpful enforcement of legal judgments. Which factor was most important? It could be claimed that it was determined individuals such as King or Johnson. On the other hand, it could be argued that violence was the greatest catalyst. The problem with the violence was that it could and did cause an eventual white backlash that effectively slowed down Johnson's reforming programme. The Kerner Report summed up the problem and demonstrated the limitations of what had been achieved:

1   What white Americans have never fully understood – but what the Negro can never forget – is that white society is deeply implicated in the ghetto. White institutions created it, white institutions maintain it, and white society condones it.... Our nation is moving toward two
5   societies, one black, one white – separate and unequal.[24]

References

1 W.T.M. Riches, *The Civil Rights Movement*, Macmillan, 1997, p. 666.
2 James Giglio, *The Presidency of John F. Kennedy*, Kansas, 1991, p. 169.
3 Hugh Brogan, *Kennedy*, Longman, 1996, p. 165.
4 Giglio, pp. 180–1.
5 Robert Dallek, *Lone Star Rising: Lyndon Johnson and his Times – 1908–1960*, Oxford University Press, 1991, p. 8.
6 Ibid., p. 137.
7 Ibid., p. 174.
8 *Houston Post*, 29 June 1986.
9 Ibid., p. 584.

10 Robert Dallek, *Flawed Giant: Lyndon Johnson and his Times – 1961–1973*, Oxford University Press, 1998, p. 24.
11 Ibid., p. 113.
12 Ibid., pp. 111–2.
13 Ibid., p. 120.
14 Irving Bernstein, *Guns or Butter: The Presidency of Lyndon Johnson*, Oxford, 1996, p. 80.
15 *Flawed Giant*, pp. 218–20.
16 Ibid., p. 236.
17 Ibid., p. 222.
18 Bernstein, p. 386.
19 *Flawed Giant*, p. 517.
20 Ibid., p. 328.
21 Bernstein, p. 499.
22 Vaughn Davis Bornet, *The Presidency of Lyndon B Johnson*, Kansas, 1983, p. 329.
23 Robert Cook, *Sweet Land Of Liberty?* Longman, 1998, p. 250.
24 John White, *Black Leadership In America*, Longman, 1994, p. 169.

Summary Diagram

PROGRESS TOWARD GREATER EQUALITY

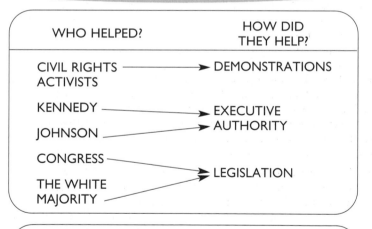

WHO HELPED?	HOW DID THEY HELP?
CIVIL RIGHTS ACTIVISTS	DEMONSTRATIONS
KENNEDY	EXECUTIVE AUTHORITY
JOHNSON	
CONGRESS	LEGISLATION
THE WHITE MAJORITY	

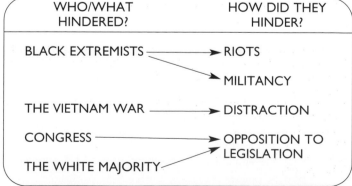

WHO/WHAT HINDERED?	HOW DID THEY HINDER?
BLACK EXTREMISTS	RIOTS
	MILITANCY
THE VIETNAM WAR	DISTRACTION
CONGRESS	OPPOSITION TO LEGISLATION
THE WHITE MAJORITY	

Working on Chapter 6

Your notes could centre on a date list of civil rights legislation (and failed attempts), with explanations of why an act was (or was not) passed. That way, you could evaluate who or what was helping or hindering most, whether the president, Congress, activists, rioters or the Vietnam War.

Answering structured and essay questions on Chapter 6

Think about this question:
How significant were the 1964 Civil Rights Act, 1965 Voting Rights Act, and 1968 Civil Rights Act?

'How significant' questions require you to look at the situation before and compare it with the situation afterwards. They invite you to weigh up results: good, bad, or insignificant!
You are now getting to the point when you can answer questions that cover a very long period. For example:

1 In what ways did the methods used by opponents of the improvement of black civil rights change from 1860–1968?
2 In what ways did opposition to the improvement of black civil rights differ between the old Confederate States and the rest of the United States, 1865–1968?

To answer '100 year questions' you need to start making notes that cover a particular aspect of race relations (here, opposition to black improvement) over the whole period. You need to ensure that your answer gives due weight to each period. You could use the chapters of this book as a general guideline. You might do one paragraph on opposition to improvement 1860s–1900, a second for 1900–45, a third for 1945–60, and maybe two for the 1960s which was such a crucial decade.

Answering source-based questions on Chapter 6

Read the source extracts on pages 114–115, 118–121 and 123–129 and think about these questions:

a) Name two 'ghettos' (page 128) (2 marks)
b) Compare and contrast the speeches of Kennedy (page 115) and Johnson (pages 123–125) on the 'moral issue'. (3 marks)
c) Account for the apparent disagreement (page 132) between Johnson

himself and Thurgood Marshall in assessing Johnson's achievements. (*4 marks*)

d) Using the sources and your own knowledge, explain why Johnson's private and public utterances on questions of race frequently differed. (*5 marks*)

e) Using the sources and your background knowledge, explain why there was opposition to the civil rights movement in the 1960s. (*10 marks*)

When looking at sources, ask yourself about the author/speaker's motivation, past history and audience. In (c), ask yourself whether Johnson has real reason to be modest, whether he was usually modest, whether he was hoping to be contradicted, etc. Is Marshall genuinely grateful, seeking promotion, or being sympathetic? Or is he simply right?

7 American Race Relations 1968–2000

POINTS TO CONSIDER

In this chapter, you have to consider not only the last quarter of the twentieth century, but also all the centuries covered by this book. You need to consider the current situation of the ethnic groups upon whom we have concentrated most. What impact has the black civil rights agitation and legislation had on blacks, Native Americans and Hispanic Americans? Finally, we have now looked at nearly 500 years of North American race relations. You need to decide the extent to which American race relations had been transformed by the year 2000. The first white settlers brought racial tensions to the continent. To what extent do they still exist?

KEY DATES

1969 Native Americans occupied Alcatraz.

1971 Supreme Court said school desegregation should be fully implemented, and supported affirmative action.

1972 Equal Employment Opportunity Act.

1982 Supreme Court said taxation powers an essential part of Indian sovereignty.

1988 Civil Rights Restoration Act countered Supreme Court erosion of effectiveness of civil rights laws.
Jesse Jackson made a serious attempt to become Democratic presidential candidate.

1990 Bush vetoed legislation to help minorities.

1991 Rodney King incident.

1995 Supreme Court attacked school desegregation.
Black Muslim Louis Farrakhan's Million Man March on Washington DC, demonstrated black males' concern for social issues and their racial pride.

With the death of Martin Luther King, the civil rights movement finally lost the sense of being a national movement. Organised direct action ended. Although Jim Crow had been destroyed, the problems of inner-city deprivation, drug abuse, rural poverty, job discrimination, unstable families, and segregated schools remained. Such problems were not confined to blacks. America's Hispanics and Native Americans were equally poor. How did Americans try to solve these problems in the last quarter of the twentieth century? Violence proved ineffective. The Black Panthers, the most famous of black 'terrorist' groups, were crushed by the FBI. More successful solutions were increased ethnic minority participation in American politics and federal intervention. The extent of federal intervention depended greatly upon presidential policies.

1 Presidential Policies

> **KEY ISSUES** How much have recent presidents helped minorities? What were their attitudes and policies?

a) President Nixon

Richard Nixon is one of America's most reviled presidents (his 'crime' was to get caught lying about a break-in of Democrat offices). Historians such as Manning Marable believe the forces of racial inequality won a major victory with Nixon's election in 1968. Others are less convinced.[1]

Nixon's record on civil rights was a strange mixture. Compared to his contemporaries, he had been exceptionally liberal on civil rights issues during the 1950s. However, he had a dim view of blacks, privately adjudging that 'there has never in history been an adequate black nation, and they are the only race of which this is true'. As president, Nixon did not want to meet black leaders and opposed the proposal that Martin Luther King's birthday should be a national holiday. Nixon crushed black radicals like the Black Panthers. He attempted a revision of the Voting Rights Act in order win the white Southern vote. He nominated an unimpressive Southern racist to the Supreme Court (a Nixon supporter contended that as many Americans were mediocre, they should have a representative on the court). He refused to back the Supreme Court when it said it was time for school desegregation to be fully implemented (SWANN v. CHARLOTTE-MECKLENBURG, 1971). That necessitated busing children considerable distances in order to ensure racially mixed schools, which Nixon considered bad for the child and the local community. However, the courts continued to endorse busing. So, whereas 68% of Southern black children attended segregated schools in the first year of Nixon's presidency, it was only 8% by the time he left the White House. Busing made Southern schools amongst America's best integrated by 1972, despite Nixon's funding of white segregationist private schools.

On the other hand, Nixon set up the Office of Minority Business Enterprise to encourage black capitalism, and embraced 'affirmative action' (or 'reverse discrimination' as its critics described it). Why? He believed jobs were the way out of the ghetto. The NAACP had flooded the EEOC with protests over employment discrimination, so Nixon's 1972 Equal Employment Opportunity Act gave EEOC greater powers of enforcement through the courts. Nixon fought off congressional and trade union opposition to help ensure that over

300,000 companies with federal contracts employed a number of blacks proportionate to the size of the population. The Supreme Court supported affirmative action in GRIGG v. DUKE POWER COMPANY (1971).

Thus the civil rights movement retained sufficient support in the courts, the federal bureaucracy, Congress and even a reluctant Nixon White House to facilitate further progress in school desegregation, employment discrimination and voting rights. Although Nixon sometimes tried to totally turn back the tide, it proved too strong. His administration tried to undermine the Great Society agencies but nevertheless dramatically increased federal expenditure on poverty programmes. Although Nixon said he hated having to pretend any sympathy for 'all that welfare crap', social security and welfare payments doubled during his presidency. Statistics suggest federal antipoverty efforts helped raise black living standards. 87% of blacks were below the poverty line in 1940, 50% in 1960, down to 30% in 1974. The civil rights movement had aimed to effect greater federal intervention on behalf of blacks. They had succeeded.

b) President Carter

Was the first Southern president since Woodrow Wilson a racist? Jimmy Carter grew up in segregated Georgia. He did not challenge segregation in his younger days. He claimed subsequently that he had been naively unaware. When campaigning to be governor of Georgia he opposed busing but, as governor, declared segregation was over and employed many blacks. While campaigning for the presidency, he declared he had 'nothing against' a community 'trying to maintain the ethnic purity of their neighbourhoods', which prompted Jesse Jackson to call him a Hitlerian throwback.[2]

As president, Carter appointed more blacks and Hispanics to the federal judiciary than any previous president. The percentage of black federal judges rose from 4% in 1977 to 9% in 1981. Carter made significant minority appointments. He appointed black women to his cabinet and made Andrew Young US ambassador to the United Nations. He renewed the Voting Rights Acts, ensured minority-owned companies had their fair share of government contracts, and deposited federal funds in minority-owned banks. He increased Justice Department power over voting rights, strengthened the EEOC, and supported the Supreme Court over BAKKE (see page 144).

c) President Reagan

As a student, Reagan supported integration of the college football team. When working as a sports broadcaster he favoured integrated baseball. However, Reagan's pre-presidential political career was not encouraging for ethnic minorities. He attacked President Johnson's civil rights legislation and the desegregation of schools and housing. When campaigning to be governor of California in 1966 he got on well with the right-wing extremist John Birch Society. However, when attacked for not supporting the 1964 Civil Rights Act, he shouted, 'I resent the implication that there is any bigotry in my nature. Don't anyone ever imply that.' He urged job training for ghetto youths to counter 'dependency culture'. Campaigning for the presidency in 1976, he explicitly linked exploitative blacks with expensive welfare financed by white taxpayers. He said Chicago's Linda Taylor had

> 80 names, 30 addresses, 12 Social Security cards and [she] is collecting veterans' benefits on four non-existing husbands.... Her tax-free cash income alone is over $150,000.[3]

He exaggerated. When Taylor got convicted of welfare fraud (1977), it was only for using two names to collect 23 welfare cheques worth $8000. The *New York Times* recorded Reagan as using the racist epithet 'young buck' when telling a Southern white audience about a young black male receiving food stamp benefit.

Although Abernathy and other black leaders supported Reagan's presidential campaign, he had little time for them once elected. He refused to speak at the NAACP annual convention in 1980 because of a prior engagement – a riding holiday. When he attended the NAACP convention in July 1981, he infuriated his audience when he said black problems were due to Democrats like Lyndon Johnson:

> 1 Many in Washington over the years have been more dedicated to making the needy people government dependent, rather than independent ... They've created a new kind of bondage. Just as the Emancipation Proclamation freed black people 118 years ago, today we
> 5 need to declare an economic emancipation.[4]

Reagan's budget director boasted that the 'Reagan Revolution' launched 'a frontal assault on the American welfare state', because welfare programmes were 'family-destroyers' which 'subsidise[d] a culture of poverty, dependency, and social irresponsibility'. Such attacks on 'welfare dependency' were not limited to whites. Ralph Abernathy declared welfare 'a mill stone around the neck of the black population'. Reagan sacked the head of the US Commission on Civil Rights (a conservative Republican appointed by Richard Nixon!) and appointed an anti-welfare conservative black Republican. Reagan did little to help the poor of any colour. Under Reagan, America's richest 5% increased their earnings by 37%, while the poorest 10% had theirs cut by 10%.

In 1982 Reagan supported Bob Jones University, South Carolina, when it challenged the Internal Revenue Service (IRS) right to deny tax exemption to segregated schools (something the three previous presidents had supported). Bob Jones University admitted a few minority students but prohibited interracial dating and marriage on biblical grounds! Reagan backed off when faced with a black outcry. He unsuccessfully opposed the Civil Rights Restoration Act of 1988. Congressional Republicans voted with Democrats to override his veto on the act. The act countered a Supreme Court ruling (GROVE CITY v. BELL, 1984) that had eroded the effectiveness of four major civil rights laws. As it was, some consider the 1988 act 'the most significant civil rights legislation in 20 years'.[5]

According to the historian W.T.M. Riches, in the same way that Lyndon Johnson caught the liberal spirit of the 1960s, Reagan 'personified, and exploited' the conservative 'fears of a nation that had been transformed by the civil rights revolution'.[6] Interestingly, Reagan had the support of many middle class blacks.

d) President Bush

Republican presidential candidate George Bush used a TV commercial linking race and crime to defeat his liberal opponent, Massachusetts governor Michael Dukakis. The 'Willie Horton' TV commercial depicted convicted black murderer Willie Horton leaving prison on furlough, thanks to Governor Dukakis, and emerging to rape and murder a white woman. Many historians think the advertisement stirred up racial fears for political gain, and helped Bush win the presidency.[7] When the Bush aide who masterminded the Willie Horton advertisement was dying of a brain tumour in 1990, he apologised for its exploitation of American racial fears.

In 1990 Bush vetoed a bill which countered Supreme Court decisions which made it difficult to prove job discrimination. According to the historian Steven Shull, Bush's veto 'represented the first defeat of a major civil rights bill in the last quarter century'.[8] Also in 1990 he vetoed a bill designed to help Native Americans.

Bush, like Reagan, nominated conservative judges to the Supreme Court. The black conservative Clarence Thomas replaced the retiring Thurgood Marshall. Thomas had entered Yale Law School through affirmative action but nevertheless opposed the policy and advocated black self-help. Thomas said he would never 'play the race card', although when a fellow black conservative accused him of sexual harassment, Thomas indicated the outcry owed much to racism. He was soon nicknamed 'Uncle Tom Justice' when he supported Supreme Court attacks on school desegregation (FREEMAN v. PITTS, 1992, and MISSOURI v. JENKINS, 1995). Thomas opposed Bush's proposed broadening of the Voting Rights Act.

e) President Clinton

Clinton gave blacks many high-level posts in his administration. He extended the Voting Rights Act, although states still remained reluctant to carry it out. He tried, but failed, to get better health care legislation (which would have helped ethnic minorities) through Congress.

2 Black Involvement in Politics

> **KEY ISSUE** What effect had the civil rights movement had upon black involvement in politics?

a) Black Organisations

Blacks continued to try to influence the political process through organisations such as the NAACP, which continued lobbying and litigation. The NAACP launched school desegregation suits and backed integration orders. However, some blacks criticised busing. They worried about the loss of black cultural cohesion. They suggested that more resources for black schools was preferable to complex busing and less likely to cause a white backlash. The most ferocious backlash came from Irish Americans in Boston, who in 1974 set up alternative schools, and used protest marches and sit-ins! Across America there was a growth in private education and a white exodus from the cities to the suburbs. In 1974 the Supreme Court overturned a Detroit busing plan by 5 to 4 (MILLIKEN v. BRADLEY). Four out of the 5 judges were Nixon appointees.

Other NAACP activities were less controversial and more clearly successful. NAACP was the most important black organisation in the Leadership Conference on Civil Rights, which represented blacks, Hispanics, women, the disabled and the elderly, and lobbied powerfully in Washington, for example, over the Voting Rights Act (1981–2).

b) Black Politicians

Now securely within the Democratic Party, blacks used the vote to gain political power. In 1972 Andrew Young was elected to Congress. Birmingham had its first black mayor in 1979, Chicago in 1983. 80% of Chicago's poorest blacks turned out to vote, suggesting that civil rights activists had ended their apathy (see page 101) after all. Although black advancement should not be exaggerated (in 1980 only 1% of America's elected officials were black) the magnitude of black political progress is best illustrated by the career of Jesse Jackson.

c) Jesse Jackson

Jesse Jackson was the son of an illiterate South Carolina sharecropper. As a student he was involved in the Greensboro sit-ins. After leaving the Chicago Theological Seminary, he headed SCLC's successful

Operation Breadbasket in Chicago in the 1960s. He hoped to be Martin Luther King's successor. He advertised their closeness. On the day of King's assassination, Jackson infuriated SCLC by appearing on TV claiming to have King's blood on his shirt and to have been the last to speak to him. Abernathy disciplined Jackson in 1971 for financial impropriety in helping black businessmen. Jackson left SCLC and set up his own organisation, 'People United to Save Humanity' (PUSH). The 'save' was quickly and modestly changed to 'serve'! PUSH used black buying power to gain black employment.

Jackson campaigned for the Democratic presidential nomination in 1984 and 1988. His appeal owed much to fears of and antagonism toward Republican President Reagan's cutbacks in welfare spending. In 1980 blacks constituted 11.7% of America's population, but 43% of those receiving Aid to Families with Dependent Children. Welfare cuts, coupled with the Reagan Justice Department's opposition to affirmative action, led many blacks to support Jackson. Other black leaders such as Andrew Young, however, did not support Jackson, whom they considered to be an unrepresentative egotist. They believed he was not the best Democrat to defeat Ronald Reagan. They disliked his alliance with controversial black nationalist Louis Farrakhan, his preference for Arabs rather than Jews, and his reference to New York City as 'Hymietown' (Jew-town). Nevertheless, Jackson was 1984's third most popular Democratic candidate. He won 20% of his support from whites. Jackson did even better in 1988 because he worked more with the Democratic Party establishment and took care to appeal more to white liberals. He doubled his vote, and 40% of his supporters were whites. His 'rainbow [all colours] coalition' appeal was demonstrated when he won 60% of New York's Hispanic vote. He came a close second to the eventual Democratic candidate.

3 Conclusions About Black Progress

> **KEY ISSUE** How far had blacks progressed by 2000?

Jesse Jackson's serious bid for the presidency demonstrates how far blacks had progressed in American politics since Martin Luther King. Blacks were mayors of major cities, and controlled parts of the Deep South. On the other hand, there was not a single black American senator in November 1999. Furthermore, political involvement alone did not solve all black problems. Lowndes County, Alabama, for example, was a great political success story, but the fifth poorest American county in 1980. Although affirmative action had helped make one third of blacks middle-class, black poverty increased in the later 1970s and 1980s because of American economic problems, Reaganite policies and increasing numbers of one parent black families. In the 1960s, 75% of black families included a husband and a wife, but by the 1990s, females headed over half of black families. The black infant mortality rate of 19% was higher than that in some Third World countries. In 1990, one third of blacks and half of all black children lived below the poverty line. Another one third had low status, low skilled jobs in low wage occupations. Average black earnings were 56% lower than white earnings, compared to 49% lower in 1975. Blacks constituted around 12% of America's population, but furnished 43% of arrested rapists, 55% of those accused of murder, and 69% of those arraigned for robbery. Whites perceived blacks as responsible for the majority of crimes. In 1994, a young black male in search of drug money mugged 81 year-old Rosa Parks in her Detroit home.

Even black mayors such as Tom Bradley of Los Angeles could not solve the problem of ghetto crime, poverty and unemployment. Why? They could not alienate white liberals by favouring blacks. They had to co-operate with the whites who dominated the local economy. Furthermore, some blacks, such as Reagan's head of the EEOC, Clarence Thomas, became critical of liberal policies and 'welfare dependency'. They echoed Booker T. Washington in emphasising self-help. Republican President George Bush appointed Thomas, the son of Georgia sharecropper, to the Supreme Court. Thomas and the other Supreme Court conservatives worked to erode affirmative action, although a 1991 Civil Rights Act overturned one of their decisions.

Black progress was thus limited by black divisions, the white backlash, and the financial and social problems associated with getting blacks out of the ghetto poverty trap. The lack of progress owed much to racial tensions, and contributed to more tension.

The violence that erupted in South Central Los Angeles in 1992 demonstrated how black and white race relations remained poor. A white man videoed four white policemen using unnecessary force to arrest black Rodney King in March 1991. A white jury exonerated the policemen in spring 1992, and in the ensuing four days of rioting, 47 people died, 2100 were injured, and 9000 arrested. The riots reflected black perceptions of an unfair legal system, and were also a result of the Reagan/Bush cuts – 40% in community funding and social service programmes, 63% in job training, and 82% in subsidised housing. Some of the violence was directed against Korean shopkeepers who were accused (like the Jews in the 1960s) of exploiting poor black customers. President Bush blamed the rioters. His Democratic successor, Bill Clinton, also failed to do anything to help ghetto blacks. His plans to improve welfare and healthcare were blocked by the Republican Congress.

While whites were reconciled to equal black legal and political rights, and appreciative of black cultural and sporting contributions to American life, widespread racism and class prejudice remained. If the solution to black poverty was higher taxation, whites did not want to know. Housing and schooling remained effectively segregated. Although Southern blacks were integrated into the political process, there was a tendency for the Democrats to be the party of Southern blacks, and Republicans of Southern whites. Racial divisions in America were well illustrated by the 1994 trial of black footballer-turned-movie-star O.J. Simpson. A predominantly black jury found Simpson innocent of murdering his estranged white wife and her lover. Black Americans applauded the verdict, while most whites considered it farcical.

The black gains and disorders of the 1960s, coupled with affirmative action, led to a great white backlash. After Richard Nixon had encouraged affirmative action, universities often gave priority to minority applicants. During the Carter presidency, marine veteran Allan Bakke challenged the University of California at Davis for rejecting his application to medical school, while minority candidates with lower scores gained places. The Californian Supreme Court ruled in his favour, but the Supreme Court (BAKKE v. REGENTS OF THE UNIVERSITY OF CALIFORNIA, 1978) upheld the university's affirmative action. Despite that setback, the white backlash continued and gained strength. For example, the state of California virtually ended affirmative action in 1999. Sometimes the white backlash verged on illegality. The 1980s and 1990s saw the revival of Ku Klux Klan-style organisations, such as the Aryan Nations that demanded a 'white homeland' in the Northwest.

In 1968 the Kerner report warned Americans they were 'moving towards two societies, one black, one white – separate and unequal'. As far as the present writer can see, after frequent visits to the United States, they continue to move that way.

4 The Red Spin-off from the Black Civil Rights Movement

> **KEY ISSUES** In what ways were the black and red situations similar and different? To what extent did the black civil rights movement influence Indians? How successful were Indian protests? How and why had the Indians' situation improved in the last quarter of the twentieth century?

While Indian reservation 'termination' (see page 74) had few defenders by 1960, the poverty, unemployment, poor housing and education on the remaining reservations was an embarrassment to the world's richest nation. Even more than blacks, Native Americans had inferior housing and education, and acute economic problems. Half of the

700,000 Native American population lived short, hard lives on the reservations, wherein employment ranged from 20% to 80%, and where, in the 1970s, life expectancy was 44 years compared to the national average of 64 years. Tuberculosis continued to kill thousands. Unlike African Americans, Native Americans had an exceptionally high suicide rate. One of the main reasons for this was that Native Americans felt their unique culture as well as their ethnicity was despised by whites.

Native Americans were inspired by the African American campaign for equality and racial unity. The National Congress of American Indians (NCAI) was established in 1944. It was the first pan-Indian movement. In 1958 NCAI helped to stop the Eisenhower administration terminating reservation rights. It won Kennedy's promise of more jobs on reservations. NCAI copied NAACP's litigation strategy, suing state and federal governments over discrimination in employment and schooling, and also for breaking treaties. In PASSAMAQUODOY v. MORTON (1972), a tribe in Maine gained massive compensation from the federal government for the latter's abrogation of a 1790 treaty. Unlike NAACP, NCAI did not seek integration into American society. It worked for the survival of the separate Native American cultural identity.

Like African Americans, Native Americans became increasingly militant in the 1960s and 1970s. Their main target was the white-dominated Bureau of Indian Affairs (BIA), which had dictatorial powers over the reservations. NCAI leaders who co-operated with the BIA were despised as 'Apples' (red on the outside but white on the inside) or 'Uncle Tomahawks' (a variant on the African American 'Uncle Tom'). In 1969, 14 Native Americans occupied Alcatraz Island, the former federal prison in San Francisco Bay. They wanted to make it a Native American Museum. Altogether, over 10,000 Native Americans visited Alcatraz during the occupation. Inspired by the black example, a Red Power movement developed. Some tribes occupied federal land. The Passamaquoddy collected tolls on a busy highway that crossed their land. Most militant of all was the American Indian Movement (AIM). AIM developed in one of the few Native American big city ghettos, in Minneapolis-St Paul. When young AIM members monitored police racism, the Native American population in the local jails dropped by 60%. AIM worked to improve ghetto housing, education and employment, then gained members from the reservations. In their first national convention AIM stressed positive imagery, and attacked white Americans' use of names such as 'Washington Redskins' (football team) and 'Atlanta Braves' (baseball team). 'Even the name Indian is not ours. It was given to us by some dumb honky [white] who got lost and thought he'd landed in India'. Indians increasingly preferred the name 'Native American'. AIM participated in a Native American March on Washington. AIM activists occupied BIA offices (1972). The violence and destructiveness in

AIM's 1972 occupation of BIA offices upset many other Native Americans, and alienated many whites.

Much Native American militancy was inspired by the African American example. White reactions to Native Americans and African Americans were frequently similar. When AIM occupied reservations, the Nixon administration used the same laws against them as were used against the Black Panthers. Although polls demonstrated white American sympathy for the Native Americans (whom they considered to be far less threatening than African Americans), most Americans were tired of demonstrations, and the Native Americans got little more than the sympathy. To a certain extent, like blacks, Native Americans were victims of the white backlash. However, as with African American activism (and perhaps partly because of African American activism), increased Native American assertiveness helped change the government's attitude. That changed attitude was the major reason for the improvement of the Indians' situation in the last quarter of the nineteenth century.

Presidents Johnson and Nixon advocated economic and political self-determination for Indians. Johnson said,

> We must affirm the right of the first Americans to remain Indians ...
> [and] their right to freedom of choice and self-determination.[9]

Talk of economic self-determination was unrealistic for many of the tribes who lacked the necessary population and land-base. Nixon therefore said,

> we must make clear that Indians can become independent of Federal control without being cut off from Federal concern and Federal support.[10]

Indian gains were sometimes the result of federal policies rather than their own increased activism. Between 1946 and 1978, the Indian Claims Commission, created by Congress, gave $800 million to Indians to compensate for previous unjust land loss. That money contributed to tribal economic development. Like blacks, Indians were amongst the greatest beneficiaries of Johnson's War on Poverty. However, as with blacks, there were Indians who disliked the resulting 'welfare dependency' culture. Indians had to rely heavily upon federal job creation schemes on the reservations. Private industry found reservations unattractive with their limited pool of skilled workers, poor communications, and distance from markets. It was neither the federal government nor Native American activism but the unique Native American culture which attracted tourist interest. Tourism proved increasingly lucrative, although from the 1970s to the 1990s the present writer witnessed many Indians who clearly resented being 'on display' to inquisitive outsiders with cameras. Jobs and rights on reservations were issues unique to Native Americans. By the end of the twentieth century, Indians dominated the Bureau of Indian Affairs (BIA) and became as effective (proportionately) as blacks in lobbying Congress. However, tribal sovereignty for America's two million Indians was a contentious issue. Tribes saw self-government as essential to the improvement of the situation. Tribes took over several functions of the federal government. They rejected state police jurisdiction on tribal land, refused to collect state taxes, and issued car licence plates. Tribal sovereignty was assisted by the Indian Self-Determination and Education Act (1975). The act encouraged tribes to manage their own affairs while retaining their special wardship status with the federal government. The rulings of Supreme Court Justice Marshall (1831–2) proved important precedents for Native American claims to tribal sovereignty. Marshall had described them as 'domestic, dependent nations'. He said states had no right to infringe upon tribal territory or authority. However, in the OLIPHANT decision (1978) and DURO v. REINA (1990), the Supreme Court limited tribal authority over non-Indians and Indians of other tribes on the reservations. Whereas the Supreme Court declared 'the power to tax is an essential attribute of Indian sovereignty' (MERRION, 1982), states such as Oklahoma resented the loss of tax revenues occasioned by around 300 Indian 'smoke shops' wherein the state tax on cigarettes was not levied. Similarly, gambling on Indian reservations upset vested white interests, as with the city of Las Vegas's opposition to gambling on Californian Indian reservations. White/red clashes over water and fishing rights were similarly controversial. It could thus be claimed that while the Native American situation had greatly improved during the twentieth century, racial tensions remained, and, as so often in the past, land ownership was a root cause.

5 The Impact of the Civil Rights Movement on Hispanic Americans and Asian Americans

> **KEY ISSUE** How did the situation of Hispanic and Asian Americans compare to that of African and Native Americans in the late twentieth century?

For many years, Mexican Americans worked and lived in isolated rural communities or in their urban ghettos. As in Mexico itself, Mexican Americans wanted little to do with the federal government. However, when in the 1960s Americans became more aware of the rights and problems of minorities, Mexican Americans began to follow the black example. Cesar Chavez's agricultural workers' labour union mirrored A. Philip Randolph's encouragement of black political awareness through union organisation. The Brown Berets modeled themselves on the Black Panthers, but compared to blacks,

Mexican Americans as a whole were less interested in and knowledgeable about such political movements and politics as a whole. They despised the 'Anglo' government that had taken the Far West from Mexico, and had discriminated against them. Interestingly, the ethnic groups that have made the most remarkable economic advances in the face of racial prejudice and legal discrimination are those who have deliberately avoided political involvement – the Japanese Americans and Chinese Americans.

6 Where Are We Now?

Throughout history, race has contributed to tension and war. Race relations therefore matter. Perhaps more than any other country, America has been home to a mixture of races. Sometimes Americans have talked optimistically of their country as the great 'melting pot'. Has the melting pot worked? Can it ever work? What lesson can be learned about race relations from the American experience?

For 500 years, American race relations have been tense. Whites dispossessed, despised and segregated Native Americans who now live in comparative poverty, trying to revitalise their culture. Whites imported, enslaved, then slowly 'freed' blacks from enslavement and political and legal inequality. African Americans however, like Native Americans, remain economically inferior and demonstrate signs of cultural disorientation. The Hispanic minority is equally 'poor' by American standards. We have seen that the causes of racial tension often appear to have been primarily economic and cultural. However, the economic rivalry between whites of different cultures (Catholic Irish Americans v. Protestant Americans) was overcome within decades, so that it may be that difference in colour is a prime cause of antagonism.

American methods of racial control have been varied. Blacks were enslaved, then when they were freed, they were subjected to *de jure* discrimination in the South and *de facto* discrimination in the North. Southern blacks were legally disfranchised and segregated. Northern blacks suffered social segregation, although it was not enshrined in law. All too frequently, violence was used to ensure black subservience. Native Americans were segregated on reservations, and their culture was attacked. Sometimes the halting of immigration or enforced emigration were used for racial control, as with Hispanics and Asian Americans. Has racial control worked? The minorities remain, and some of them have prospered. *De jure* discrimination (as in the South) proved easier to combat than *de facto* discrimination, but theoretically there is no racial discrimination in the politically correct America of today. However, the legacy of racial tension lingers on and the tension is self-perpetuating.

The results of racial antagonism might seem to be economic problems, judging from the relative poverty of many African American, Native Americans, and Hispanic Americans. However, as we have seen, Asian Americans were frequently made unwelcome in North America, yet they have progressed to economic equality – even superiority. Similarly, while racial antagonism can lead to cultural disorientation, some victims of racism either adapt to the dominant white American culture or quite happily retain their own. It would seem then that the history of American race relations serves only to prove that people of different races struggle to get along with each other, but that some adapt and survive with greater ease and less pain than others. The differentiating factors seem to be historical experience (such as slavery) and/or cultural adaptability.

References

1 Robert Cook, *Sweet Land of Liberty?*, Longman, 1998, pp. 252–3.
2 Burton Kaufman, *The Presidency of James Earl Carter, Jr*, Kansas, 1993, p. 13.
3 W.T.M. Riches, *The Civil Rights Movement*, Macmillan, 1997, p. 113.
4 Ibid., p. 114.
5 Steven Shull, quoted in Riches, p. 119.
6 Ibid., p. 119.
7 Ibid., pp. 163–4.
8 Ibid., p. 166.
9 Quoted in William T. Hagan, *American Indians*, The University of Chicago Press, 1993, p. 186.
10 Ibid., p. 186.

Summary Diagram

	AFRICAN AMERICANS	NATIVE AMERICANS	HISPANIC AMERICANS	ASIAN AMERICANS
Poorer than average?	YES	YES	YES	NO
Worse living conditions than average?	YES	YES	YES	NO
Worse schools?	YES	YES	YES	NO
Suffering from erosion of affirmative action?	YES	n/a	YES	NO
Fairly represented in national politics?	ALMOST	TRYING TO MAINTAIN TRIBAL SOVEREIGNTY	NO	NO
Cultural disorientation?	YES e.g. increasing single-parent families	YES – but decreasingly so	YES e.g. gangs	NO
Perceived as a problem by whites?	OFTEN	OFTEN	OFTEN	ONLY OCCASIONALLY
Hostile to whites?	OFTEN	OFTEN	OFTEN	ONLY OCCASIONALLY
Hostile to other minorities?	OFTEN	OFTEN	OFTEN	ONLY OCCASIONALLY
Resented by other minorities	OFTEN	OCCASIONALLY	OFTEN	OFTEN

Working on Chapter 5

This chapter attempts to finish off the story. The real work for you is to obtain an overview of the contents of the book. You need to chart the progress (and regression) of the different ethnic groups in America, especially as examiners like to evaluate your ability to understand change and continuity over long periods. You could do summary date lists that bring out progress and regression in the history of African Americans, Native Americans, Hispanic Americans and Asian Americans. You should also look at federal and state government activity, and reasons for opposition/methods of opposition to racial equality. As always, you can use the suggested essay questions below to give you further ideas on the direction of your note taking and revision.

Answering essay questions on Chapter 5

You are now in a position to think about these essays:

1. To what extent did African Americans and Native Americans benefit from campaigns for their civil rights, 1947–2000?
2. How did African Americans attempt to improve their position in American society 1865–2000?
3. How have the federal and state governments dealt with the 'black problem' since the foundation of the United States of America?
4. In what ways have blacks faced discrimination since their first arrival in North America?
5. In what ways did opposition to the improvement in black civil rights change 1865–2000?
6. Why did whites in the Deep South oppose the improvement of the black situation 1865–2000?
7. Give reasons for the opposition to racial equality, and the effectiveness of that opposition, in American history.

Further Reading

Inevitably, there are many books available on the great mid twentieth century black civil rights movement. Two useful studies have been published recently: Robert Cook's *Sweet Land of Liberty?* (Longman, 1998) and W.T.M. Riches' *The Civil Rights Movement* (Macmillan, 1997). Even more detailed are Taylor Branch's *Parting the Waters* and *Pillar of Fire* (Simon and Schuster, 1988–98). The best biography of Martin Luther King is probably David Garrow's 800-page *Bearing the Cross* (Vintage, 1993). Stephen Oates' *Let the Trumpet Sound* (Payback, 1998) is a slightly easier but less scholarly read. John White gives an accessible overview of *Black Leadership in America* (Longman, 1994). The American presidents and the race problem are well and systematically covered in many biographies. For Truman, see Donald McCoy, *The Presidency of Harry S. Truman* (Kansas, 1984); David McCullough, *Truman* (Simon & Schuster, 1992); Alonzo Hamby, *Man of the People* (Oxford, 1995). For Eisenhower, see C.J. Pach and E. Richardson, *The Presidency of Dwight D. Eisenhower* (Kansas, 1991), and Stephen Ambrose, *Eisenhower* (Simon & Schuster, 1990). James Giglio is the best on *The Presidency of John F. Kennedy* (Kansas, 1991). Johnson is admirably served by biographers: Robert Dallek's two volume study, *Lyndon Johnson and his Times* (Oxford, 1991–8) and Irving Bernstein's *Guns or Butter* (Oxford, 1996) are both fair and immensely detailed. Stephen Ambrose's three volume *Nixon* (Simon & Schuster, 1987–1991) is excellent. Carter, Reagan, Bush and Clinton await similar coverage.

Native Americans are adequately (if not well) covered in W.T. Hagan, *American Indians* (Chicago, 1993) and Angie Debo, *A History of the Indians of the United States* (Pimlico, 1995).

The history of African Americans is amply covered, for example, in John Hope Franklin and Alfred Moss, *From Slavery to Freedom* (McGraw-Hill, 1998). It is far more difficult to obtain good, comprehensive coverage of the other ethnic minorities who have been the victims of racism, but Thomas Sowell, *Ethnic America* (Basic Books, 1981) is probably the best attempt. Peter Carroll and David Noble, *The Free and the Unfree* (Penguin, 1998) is a refreshing look at American history from the viewpoint of the less fortunate.

Index